Sharks

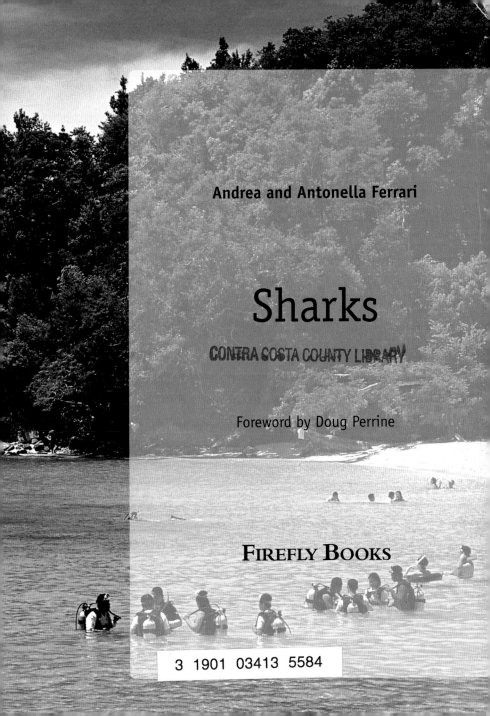

Andrea and Antonella Ferrari

Sharks

Foreword by Doug Perrine

FIREFLY BOOKS

Published by Firefly Books Ltd. 2002

First Printing 2002

Publisher Cataloging-in-Publication Data (U.S.)

Ferrari, Andrea.
    Sharks : a Firefly guide / Andrea and Antonella Ferrari. -- 1st ed.
[256] p. : col. photos. ; cm.
Includes bibliographical references and index.
Summary: A comprehensive guide to 120 species of sharks including habitat, dimensions, biology, behavior and mythology.
ISBN 1-55209-629-7 (pbk.)
1. Sharks. I. Ferrari, Antonella. II. Title.
597.3 21   CIP
QL638.9.F47 2002

National Library of Canada Cataloguing in Publication Data

Ferrari, Andrea
    Sharks : a Firefly guide
Translated from the original Italian 2000 ed., Tutto squali, by Anna Bennett.
Includes bibliographical references and index.
ISBN 1-55209-629-7
    1. Sharks. 2. Sharks— Pictorial works. I. Ferrari, Antonella II. Bennett, Anna III. Title.
QL638.9.F4813 2002
597.3   C2001-902620-X

Published in Canada in 2002 by
Firefly Books Ltd.
3680 Victoria Park Avenue
Toronto, Ontario M2H 3K1

Published in the United States in 2002 by
Firefly Books (U.S.) Inc.
P.O. Box 1338
Ellicott Station
Buffalo, New York 14205

English text edited by Maraya Raduha

Photographs:
p.1: Pulau Mabul, Malaysia
p. 2/3: Preparing to dive, Tunku Abdul Rahman Marine Park, Malaysia
p. 4/5: Blue shark, *Prionace glauca*
p. 6/7: Tiger shark, *Galeocerdo cuvier*
p. 9: Scalloped hammerhead shark, *Sphyrna lewini*
p. 240/241: Blacktip shark, *Carcharhinus limbatus*

Printed in Spain
D.L.T.O: 1333-2001

CONTENTS

Symbols

Exclusively or mainly diurnal by habit.

Exclusively or mainly crepuscular or nocturnal by habit.

May be observed by day or at night; the period of specific activity is indicated in the entry.

The first symbol indicates species that are potentially dangerous if excited or disturbed; the second, those verified as dangerous; the third, those that are *extremely dangerous,* reponsible for unprovoked attacks on swimmers and skin-divers. Only these last species may regard humans as potential prey and should therefore be approached with extreme caution.

The **species** described in the book are divided by **order**. For each species allotted an individual entry, the **common name** is followed by the **genus** and **species**, the **classifier** and the **year of classification** (e.g., **Tiger shark,** *Galeocerdo cuvier,* Peron & Le Sueur, 1822). The entry then lists the name of the **family** (Carcharhinidae) and gives details of the species' **range, habitat, size** and **habits**.

Each section is devoted to one or more orders and preceded by a four-page introduction, two comprising a double-page photograph and two with illustrated details and brief texts explaining the anatomical features of the representatives of the orders concerned. The entries dealing with Rajiformes, toward the back of the book, are separated from those describing the true sharks and are similarly preceded by a short introduction.

FOREWORD

What word comes to mind when you think of sharks? The most appropriate adjective would be "diverse." The more than 1000 species of sharks and rays have such a variety of different forms and lifestyles that it is very hard to come up with generalizations that apply to all members of the group. Yet most people think of all sharks as a single animal with characteristics so well known that most writers use exactly the same words when describing them. As the well-known artist Richard Ellis points out in his book of paintings of sharks, teeth are always "razor sharp." Dorsal fins always "slice ominously through the water." All 1000 plus elasmobranchs are lumped together as "The Shark." The public image of "The Shark" has been so well-crafted by Hollywood that Jean-Claude Van Damme's publicist should blush. In many cases the image is the opposite of reality for most species. "The Shark" is immortal and invincible. Yet most shark species are fragile and vulnerable. "The Shark" is voracious, yet most sharks eat less than more active fish and mammals. Many of these words so often used for sharks are better applied to our own kind, which has taken over the planet, crowding out and consuming most other forms of life, including sharks, whose numbers have plummeted as human populations have entered the most recent phase of explosive growth. Some species of sharks and rays are already in imminent danger of extinction due to human activities, and more will undoubtedly follow. For now though, there remains a marvelous diversity to this fascinating group. This new book by my good friends and colleagues, Andrea and Antonella Ferrari, should help the reader to appreciate the variety of interesting species within it, and to realize their grace and beauty when encountered in their natural habitats.

Doug Perrine

INTRODUCTION

LORDS OF THE DEEP

A New Image

Even today the very word "shark" provokes in us obscure fears and ancestral terrors; and the same irrational sense of danger is evoked by other creatures that are entirely different, such as snakes and wolves, although usually people who react violently and fearfully at the mere mention of these creatures have never seen them in the wild, nor are they ever likely to do so. Actually, the image of these animals, which so inexplicably chills us to the depths of our being, is little more than fantasy, a figment of the imagination derived from decades of bad adventure films, cheap fiction and tall tales unconnected to everyday reality. From the 1930s and 1940s onward, truth and fantasy have overlapped inextricably; first with the discovery and subsequent documentation, usually sensationalized, of tropical shores that had thus far remained unviolated, and then with incidents arising from the Second World War. So, although it was obviously impossible for anyone to rip open a shark with a single thrust of a knife, as was done repeatedly in the cinema, it was nonethe-

Sharks are among the most elegant of all animals. Humans fear them unjustly and have given them a bad name, alleging that they are aggressive by nature, which is not true. They are simply predators at the apex of the marine ecosystem.

less tragically true that many torpedoed sailors and bailed-out pilots—who during the war had been left at the mercy of the sea, often for days on end—had been killed by these predators while awaiting the arrival of help.

It is undeniable that certain species of tropical sharks—and also other huge predators such as the Nile and marine crocodiles—have long represented a genuine danger to people living along river banks. What, however, is important to grasp is that such sharks, stripped of the cloak of myth and superstition in which they have been wrapped by innumerable travelers and writers, are merely fish. Often of extraordinary elegance and beauty, sometimes astonishingly evolved, in some cases capable of inflicting grave wounds with their spectacular teeth, yet, at the same time simply fish, unable to show human-type feelings such as malice or desire for revenge, instinctively prepared to flee if threatened, tending to be timid and difficult to approach, and often surprisingly delicate. Today, as is evident, it is actually sharks that have reason to fear humans, not the other way round.

Similarities and Differences

In what way do sharks differ from other fish? Sharks and rays are cartilaginous fishes, the Chondrichthyes, of which they form the subclass Elasmobranchii, in contrast to the Osteichthyes, or bony fishes. Like the latter, they extract the oxygen necessary for life from the surrounding water by a specialized structure of the gills, and they move by undulating the streamlined body using a combination of fins, either single (caudal, dorsal and anal) or paired (pectoral and pelvic). Many of them are carnivorous hunters, and they reproduce, depending on species, either by laying eggs or producing live young. The structural features that distinguish the Chondrichthyes are the gills (which in sharks open on the outside as simple slits, varying in number from five to seven, whereas in bony fishes they are always protected by a bony covering known as the operculum); the fins (stiff and lami-

Many of the Rajiformes, as exemplified by the photograph below of a "squadron" of eagle rays, display a graceful swimming action equal to that of the sharks, to whom they are closely related. Sharks and rays are distinguished by their cartilaginous, flexible skeletons.

nate, similar to the wings of an airplane, without bony inner rays that characterize the Osteichthyes); the skin (which in sharks consists of a layer, of variable thickness, of derma in which are embedded innumerable enameled tooth-like placoid scales, whereas in bony fishes they generally take the form of large, flat scales); and finally and most particularly, the skeleton, which is made up mainly of strong cartilage rather than hard bone as is the case with the Osteichthyes. Sharks, moreover, have no swim bladder and the majority regulate their balance in water through their highly evolved body structure and the large size of their liver, which is rich in oils. Another important distinction between the Chondrichthyes and the Osteichthyes is the general structure of the upper jaw or maxilla (as opposed to the lower jaw or mandible) which in practice is not fused to the skull. Sometimes this arrangement results in a spectacular projection of the teeth—so conspicuous in books and films devoted to the great white shark, *Carcharodon carcharias*—enabling such species to rip huge chunks of flesh from their prey.

An Incredible Variety

In other respects it is impossible to generalize. Some sharks are under 15 cm (6 in) long and others grow to more than 15 m (50 ft); yet about half of the existing 400 or so currently classified species measure less than a meter in length. Certain species are notable for their exceptional predatory capacities (tiger shark, mako, white shark, hammerhead); others feed exclusively on microscopic organisms in the form of plankton. About twenty-five species are known to have deliberately attacked humans on many occasions, but the number of attacks recorded each year throughout the world is generally less than a hundred. The most dangerous species for swimmers is probably the bull shark, *Carcharhinus leucas*, also known as the cub shark. For skin-divers, however, the most perilous species—according to the celebrated underwater explorer and author, the late Jacques-Yves Cousteau—is the oceanic whitetip shark, *Carcharhinus longimanus*. Many species, nevertheless, may turn extremely dangerous if triggered off by the phenomenon of "feeding frenzy" (typical also of tuna), during which individuals launch furious, repeated

attacks on prey such as a shoal of fish). On such occasions they are likely to attack whatever comes within their reach, including other sharks, which are sometimes wounded and devoured.

Sharks exhibit an astonishing variety of shapes, colors and habits. In the popular mind, however, the typical image of a shark is represented by the members of the order Carcharhiniformes, such as the whitetip reef shark, the tiger shark and the gray reef shark, illustrated on these pages.

A Perfect Animal

Popular culture has it that sharks are primitive and stupid, but nothing could be further from the truth. Under normal conditions, sharks behave with quite a measure of intelligence, and various experiments have shown that their learning capacity compares with that of rats and birds. Moreover, the fact that present-day sharks, which exhibit an astonishing range of diversity, have not changed substantially for the last 150 million years (with the oldest going back 350 million years) suggests they have attained a level of evolution that approaches perfection. They are consummate predators (equipped with as many as 3,000 teeth, arranged in five rows); incomparable swimmers (the blue shark, *Prionace glauca*, migrates annually more than 3,000 km (1,860 miles)

following the Gulf Stream, while the mako shark (*Isurus*) may reach a speed of 35 kmh (21 mph); and highly prolific breeders: the female blue shark may give birth to as many as 135 young.

Sharks are exceptionally adaptable animals that have come to occupy many ecological niches, from tropical seas to the Arctic and Antarctic oceans, and are sometimes present in freshwater streams and rivers. Species may be pelagic or coastal, migratory or sedentary, midwater or benthic. However, like other highly developed animals, they have to adjust progressively to biological change (a long growth period and late sexual maturity) and hence

Contrary to what is often alleged, sharks as a rule do not launch blind attacks on all living creatures that come within their reach; in fact, they restrict themselves to a particular ecological niche, like virtually any other animal, hunting only when necessary.

need time to adapt to altered environmental conditions. Human modification of the earth's habitats at an astonishing rate is threatening the extinction of many species. During the last ten years alone humans have done more harm to present-day sharks than had been done in the 150 million years since they first appeared. Throughout their long history, sharks, which survived the age of the dinosaurs unscathed, have never faced such a grave threat to their future existence.

ORIGINS AND EVOLUTION

Mute Witness to a Distant Past

Digging up the past to discover traces of ancient animals often depends on sheer luck rather than scientific qualifications. Reconstructing the history of sharks is an even more complicated challenge largely because of their very structure, for their cartilaginous skeleton, after death,

dissolves rapidly. This does not easily create conditions conducive to fossilization, which requires considerable time for the organic matter to be gradually replaced by minerals. As far as sharks are concerned, therefore, the paleontological evidence has to be based on just a few clues: teeth, spines, scales (dermal denticles), and small portions of ossified vertebrae—the most durable parts of the body. With these elements alone students have worked to compose a puzzle that still lacks many important pieces. Yet every now and then researchers have benefited from a genuine stroke of luck. Thanks to particularly fortunate circumstances, several complete fossils of ancient species, forerunners of modern sharks, survived to this day and were discovered.

This picture of a gray reef shark, Carcharhinus amblyrhynchos, taken from below, shows clearly all the different rigid fins these fish normally have. The drawing below illustrates the external anatomy of a typical shark.

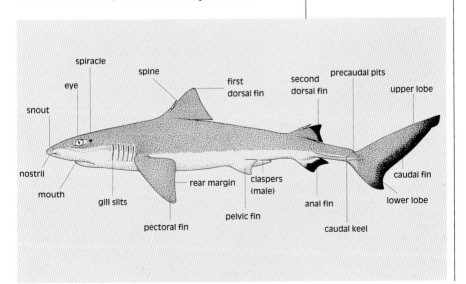

The oldest of these fossils date from around 400 million years ago, from the Devonian, a period that teemed with innumerable species of bony fishes and other marine creatures, and which saw the appearance on earth of the Chondrichthyes or cartilaginous fishes. Deriving from these extremely ancient progenitors are all the species that exist today, more than 1,100 of them, comprising the sharks and rays, which include the electric rays and chimaeras. Exactly what happened to induce the first proto-sharks to use their fins for propulsion in the immensity of the oceans 400 million years ago, we shall probably never know. The oldest complete

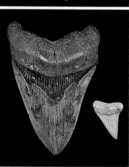

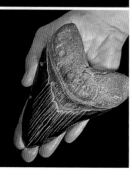

fossil of the ancestral shark, *Cladoselache*, shows a fish already well advanced in the evolutionary scale, endowed with many of the attributes of present-day sharks.

Cladoselache was a cartilaginous fish that grew to over 2 m (6.5 ft) in length and exhibited, among other anatomical features exclusive to sharks, five gill slits, a tail of typically asymmetrical structure (heterocercal), strong spines made up of enamel and dentine situated in front of the two dorsal fins, numerous teeth constituted of a shallow discoidal root and a crown, formed of a central cusp flanked by two smaller cusps. It is a structure still to be found today, with the same pattern, in many shark species. *Cladoselache* was presumably also an excellent swimmer, swift and agile, as is suggested by the form of the tail, similar to that of the great white shark and the mako, two of the most efficient swimmers among the present-day pelagic sharks. The finding of fossil specimens containing whole fish, swallowed tail first, seems to confirm the speed of these predators, who nevertheless were compelled in their turn to guard against the heavier but colossal Arthrodira, armored fish with a length of over 6 m (20 ft). The appearance of *Cladoselache* at a time when the bony fishes had already populated the seas for millions of years has led experts to a conclusion at variance with what has usually

been assumed; namely, that the cartilaginous fishes ought not to be regarded as primitive creatures in relation to the bony fishes, but, in fact, derived from the latter. Nor is it correct to maintain that the sharks are primitive in development simply because many present-day species, according to the fossil evidence, have remained practically unchanged for 150 million years. This fact, indeed, really shows how the shark "blueprint," which appeared on our planet more than 400

Facing page: some spectacular fossil teeth from the gigantic Miocene shark Carcharocles megalodon, *which measured 15 m (50 ft) long, with a detail of the serrated edge and a comparison with a tooth of the present-day great white shark,* Carcharodon carcharias. *Below: two fossilized teeth of* C. carcharias *found in Chile; above: Dr. Gordon Hubbell displays the jaws of a modern great white shark.*

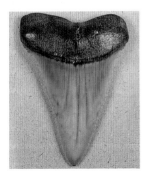

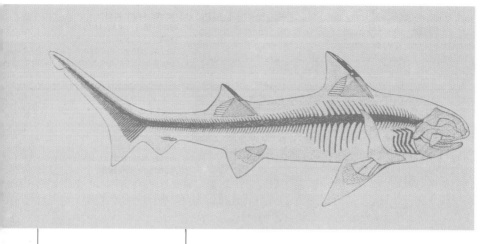

Because of their very bone structure—the cartilaginous skeleton tends to disintegrate during the process of fossilization—the Chondrichthyes have left behind very little fossil evidence.

million years ago, was already at that time superbly designed to withstand virtually any alterations to the environment, even those that were to lead to the extinction of the dinosaurs and the great marine reptiles.

The history of the Chondrichthyes is similarly marked by extinctions. *Cladoselache* and the other closely related sharks that hunted in the Devonian seas disappeared around 250 million years ago. Some of these species looked quite bizarre, often with cutting spines that reached over the cranium or with sharp cutaneous denticles above the head and on the first dorsal fin. There is no knowing what purpose these strange structures served; perhaps they enabled the fishes to attach themselves to bigger animals, rather as modern remoras (or sharksuckers) do with sharks and whales.

A Predator That Outlived the Dinosaurs

Although the Cladodontidae (*Cladoselache* and related species) eventually vanished, other more evolved sharks meanwhile made

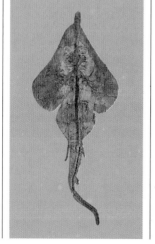

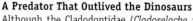

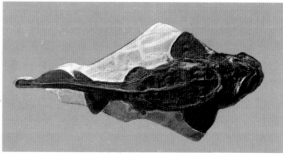

their appearance. About 400 million years ago the Xenacanthidae—primitive Condrichthyes that colonized only freshwater habitats—were already branching out. Following these, in the Carboniferous, some 320 million years ago, came the Hybodontidae. These sharks possessed a number of modern characteristics and may thus be considered the immediate ancestors of present-day sharks. For example, they had claspers, male copulatory organs. The Hybodontidae became extinct at about the same time as the dinosaurs. Yet this was during a period when modern sharks had already made an appearance, as attested by the teeth of a mako and of a mackerel shark (porbeagle) discovered in strata of the Lower Cretaceous (about 100 million years ago). The white shark, geologically speaking, arrived soon afterward; its teeth have been found in fossil layers dating back 60–65 million years. Yet these teeth are no more than one-third the length of those of a gigantic shark that then dominated the oceans of the

Facing page, above: The drawing shows a schematic reconstruction of Hybodus, *the most ancient representative of the order Selachii, representing a link with the still more primitive Cladoselachii. Species of the genus* Hybodus *lived in the oceans from the Permian to the Cretaceous era. Below: a beautiful ray from the Eocene deposit of Monte Bolca, near Verona, Italy (Bolca Museum of Fossils).*

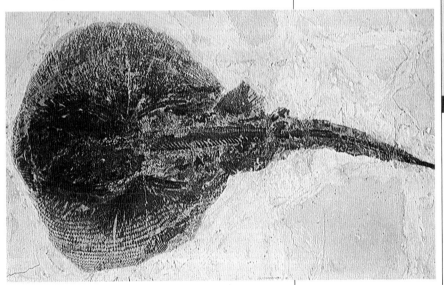

world: *Carcharodon* (or *Carcharocles*) *megalodon*. On the basis of reliable reconstructions, this leviathan of the seas measured 15–20 m (50–65 ft) long: the dimensions of an average-sized sperm whale. Experts have lately argued about the true connection between *Carcharodon megalodon* and the white shark, believed until not long ago to be closely related, if not actually representatives of the same species that, because of the gradual reduction in the size of prey, became progressively smaller. Today a new theory maintains that the two huge predators belong to different evolutionary branches and the one derived from

Fossil finds of sharks and rays are very rare. Above: a hybodontid dating from about 300 million years ago.

Reconstruction of Cladoselache, one of the first known Chondrichthyes. The anterior fins (A), with a very broad base compared with those of modern Selachii (B), would not have facilitated a speedy, agile swimming action.

Facing page, above: other interesting examples of fossilized teeth: 1) Isurus hastalis, *19 million years;* 2) Isurus planus, *19 million years;* 3) Otodus obliquus, *130 million years;* 4) Carcharocles angustidens, *28 million years;* 5) Carcharocles auriculatus, *40 million years.*

C. megalodon finally became extinct. To tangle the web even further, the discovery of enormous teeth still not wholly fossilized, at considerable ocean depths, has persuaded some scientists to conclude that the extinction of *C. megalodon* must have occurred more recently, about 2 million years ago.

Even so, there are sharks of the present day that scientists acknowledge as genuine living fossils, interesting subjects of study in order to understand and interpret the structure of their

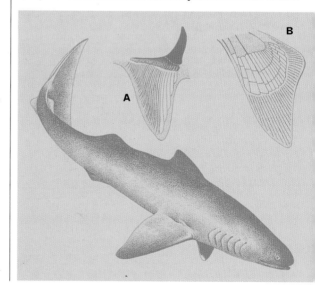

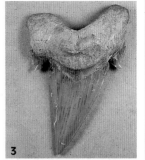

extinct predecessors. One of these is the frilled shark, *Chlamy-doselachus anguineus*, which lives at immense depths, down to 1,300 m (4,200 ft). An extreme environment has probably enabled this fish to retain ancestral features such as the long eel-like body, the presence of six gill slits, and teeth with deep cusps capable of seizing prey comparable to those of the ancient Xenacanthidae. Another characteristic of the frilled shark is the upper jaw, which is fused to the skull, unlike that of modern sharks, where it is extensible, joined to the skull by movable ligaments that allow the jaw to move forward as it bites. Other families of modern sharks that exhibit features typical of extinct ancestors, such as the Cladodontidae, Hybodontidae and Xenodontidae, are the Heterodontidae, or bullhead sharks, which live for the most part in the coral seas of the Far East and Oceania, and the Hexanchidae, widely distributed in temperate and subtropical seas, and characterized by having a variable number (six or seven) of gill slits.

The fossilized imprint of a rare Cladoselache, *ancestor of present-day sharks, which lived more than 400 million years ago.*

The barbels of nurse sharks (above) and the vomerine-nasal grooves of whitetip reef sharks (below) and zebra sharks (facing page, above) heighten the sensory functions in conditions of low visibility.

SENSE ORGANS

Ampullae of Lorenzini

Of all the shark's sense organs, arguably the most remote from our world are the ampullae of Lorenzini, which were first discovered and described by the Italian anatomist Stefano Lorenzini in the seventeenth century. The majority of these ampullae are situated in the shark's head, surrounding the eyes and alongside the lateral line system, and particularly concentrated in the "nose" region. Their structure is relatively simple. Canals, filled with a gelatinous fluid and situated deep inside the skin, terminate in a pore that opens out at the skin's surface. The end of each canal broadens to form a small saclike structure (the ampulla). At the base of this sac are a number of sensory cells connected to nerve fibers that run to the brain. The function of these structures, found only in sharks and rays (and thus uniquely developed in the Elasmobranchii), long remained a mystery. From their constitution it was obvious that the ampullae were in some way sense organs, but nobody could understand how they worked. It was initially thought that the ampullae were mechanoreceptors, whereby mechanical deformation modified the electrical discharge of the attached nerves (those leading to the brain). Other experiments, in the 1930s, made it clear that these organs were sensitive to temperature. Only in the 1960s and 1970s did other ingenious experiments demonstrate that the ampullae were capable of perceiving elec-

trical fields emitted by any animal, even if the animal is motionless. In fact, any bodily activity, especially muscular, produces very weak electrical fields that spread out in an invisible ring. Around the head of an average-sized fish, for exam-

Below: a detail of the snout of a smalleye hammerhead, Sphyrna tudes, *showing the ampullae of Lorenzini. Bottom, from top, detail of the eye of a tiger shark*, Galeocerdo cuvier *(partially covered by the nictitating membrane), the bluntnose sixgill shark*, Hexanchus griseus, *and the leopard shark*, Triakis semifasciata.

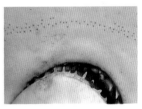

ple, an electric potential of 500 microvolts per centimeter has been registered. The ampullae of Lorenzini are capable of perceiving these minute differences of intensity.

The sensitivity of these organs is extremely high, to the extent that certain species of rays and true sharks may be aware of a difference of five-milliards (five-billionths) of a volt per centimeter. But even with this heightened measure of sensibility, the ampullae of Lorenzini are used only in particular situations because the electrical fields generated by the animals are quickly attenuated by the water, and a shark can only perceive them at a distance of a few meters. The value mentioned above, of 500 microvolts per centimeter, drops at 5 cm (2 in) to 2 microvolts per centimeter, and at 10 cm (4 in) to 0.2 microvolts per centimeter.

Such a specialized and particular sense may be diffused among species that feed on benthic animals that live on the bottom and tend to hide in the sand, such as soles, rays and some mollusks. And in fact it seems certain, from experiments carried out in the 1970s by A.J. Kalmijn, that the ampullae are employed only in the final stages of hunting, when the prey is just a few centimeters from the shark's snout. These experiments offered the predator a sole concealed in the sand, which the shark noticed only after coming in as close as 10 cm (4 in). In some special situations, as when the prey was electrically isolated, the shark remained quite unaware of its presence.

The ampullae may be used on other occasions. If the sharks can perceive electrical fields, they may be equally responsive to magnetic fields. The earth's magnetic field produces minuscule voltage charges, but far beyond the sensitivity of the ampullae

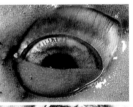

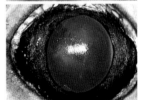

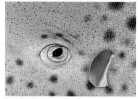

Above, from top: close-up of the eye and spiracle of a zebra shark, Stegostoma fasciatum, *of a blacktip shark,* Carcharhinus limbatus, *and of a Galapagos shark,* Carcharhinus galapagensis. *The last of these clearly shows the nictitating membrane that partly covers the pupil. Right: Antonella Ferrari approaches a large black-spotted stingray,* Taeniura melanospilos. *Rays are often endowed with excellent vision.*

of Lorenzini. A shark swimming through these magnetic fields might perceive a voltage of 0.4 microvolts per centimeter. Moreover, even underwater currents generate an electrical field, from the moment the ions contained in them move into the earth's magnetic field. Within these currents it may be possible to determine the direction of travel. Sensing the variation of the magnetic field in different areas of ocean might prove extremely useful, particularly during long migrations. The open ocean is obviously an environment without any particular features, offering no point of reference to its inhabitants. Navigating by means of the magnetic field, as has been demonstrated for certain marine turtles, is an efficient and convenient method of determining the starting and finishing points of a journey. This theory is reinforced by the fact that some sharks, such as many species of hammerheads (*Sphyrnidae*), tend to crowd around points of anomalous magnetism in the ocean.

The ampullae of Lorenzini have also been associated with other senses, such as perception of mechanical stimuli or of heat. Results of such experiments have not yet been confirmed, but perhaps these organs could also prompt the perception of comparable variations.

One curious fact relating to the magnetic awareness of sharks is the hypothesis that it may be in some way associated with the ability of some rays to deliver powerful electric shocks. These shocks, which are used to stun predators (or careless swimmers) might be designed to blunt the electric sensitivity of sharks for a few seconds, thus enabling the ray to escape capture.

Smell
The sense of smell is of paramount importance to sharks; as a group they have been described as "swimming noses." Many

species seem to rely above all on smell for locating and pursuing their prey; and the observation of shark behavior in shallow waters confirms its importance. A skin-diver who catches a fish that struggles and spills blood in the water is likely to be surrounded within seconds by sharks attempting to snatch the prey, even if visibility is poor, often with dangerous consequences for the diver. This

propensity is exploited on some barrier reefs where chunks of meat are offered as bait to attract sharks toward tourists.

Since this is the most primitive of the senses, the structure of the olfactory organ is relatively simple. An olfactory bulb is connected to a large olfactory sac concealed inside the nostrils, and from this an olfactory nervous tract extends into the front of the brain. Contrary to what happens in terrestrial vertebrates, the nostrils have a purely sensory function and are not associated with breathing. The external structure of the nostrils is fairly complex because strips of fleshy tissue force the water to flow

Above: Dr. Samuel Gruber from the University of Miami uses a liquid colorant while studying the respiratory and olfactory discharges of a nurse shark, Ginglymostoma cirratum. Below: the specialized head shape of the scalloped hammerhead, Sphyrna lewini, improves their sense of smell.

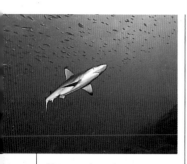

Above: an immature gray reef shark, Carcharhinus amblyrhynchos, *patrols its territory along the reef.*
Right: a tiger shark, Galeocerdo cuvier, *is directed to its prey—here the carcass of a marlin—by a complex combination of sensory stimuli.*

into one opening and out the other. Thus, the water flow is constantly renewed so that even the tiniest percentage of particles can be perceived. According to a once fashionable theory, the sensitivity of sharks was derived from their capacity to accumulate particles in the convolutions of their nasal sacs. Recent experiments, however, have proved this idea wrong, indicating that the particles may settle on the sensitive cells and exit without collecting in the nostrils. The nasal sacs likewise increase the sensitivity of smell, for they are arranged in microscopically minute folds that augment the surface of perception. The shark's sense of smell is so acute that some substances can be registered in concentrations of less than one part per million.

This high sensitivity perhaps explains a particular behavior among white sharks. During the reproductive season many individuals of this species take to living near colonies of seals and sea lions, feeding on pups or inexperienced young. At other times of the year, in the Pacific Ocean, they apparently follow whales on their migrations to the west coast of North America. Some whales die of natural causes on the journey and the white sharks can pick up the traces of the long trail left by substances given off by their decomposing bodies. It is obvious, of course, that a shark does not perceive or, more precisely, will not react

in the same way to all particles that it smells. Extensive experiments carried out by the U.S. Navy to find a shark repellent pointed to substances usually emitted by injured bodies, such as proteins present in the flesh, blood and skin of fishes and mammals. It became evident, moreover, that many of these substances stimulate different parts of a shark's brain, some apparently unconnected with smell and feeding. The most powerful

substances were shown to be amines and amino acids of the flesh, and proteins found in the blood such as hemoglobin and serum albumin.

In Pursuit of Prey

Once aware of the substance, the shark will, as a rule, follow the current with the greatest concentration, as do male moths when they pick up the scent of females. In this way the predator can arrive relatively quickly at the source of the olfactory particles. Hammerhead sharks may have attained an even higher degree of sensitivity because the nostrils are far removed to the tips of the head extensions.

Only at the moment of the actual attack does the sense of taste come into play, activated by the taste buds inside the mouth. It would seem, therefore, that taste is the final determinant in the shark's acceptance of food. Some sharks appear to be keenly sensitive to the presence of fat in the tissues of their prey. They bite whatever they can but release any animals that seem too "thin" for them. This is especially true of the white shark, which lives in comparatively cold waters. For this reason, it will readily swallow a captured seal or sea lion, but will spit out sea birds and humans that do not contain sufficient fat for its liking.

The whitetip reef shark, Triaenodon obesus, *has a deceptively lazy appearance, but it is an active hunter at night, relying above all on its sense of smell and its electroreceptive organs.*

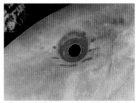

An Excellent Repellent

Studies into ways of deterring sharks almost invariably aim at the discovery of substances that have an effect on the sense of smell. An extremely interesting channel of research has focused on a compound present in the flesh of a Red Sea sole, *Pardachirus marmoratus*. This species avoids the bite of a shark by secreting a detergent substance called pardaxin, which harms the cell membranes. It seems that this substance, or others that are similar, functions only if injected directly into the shark's mouth.

Vision

Having considered the shark's remarkable sense of smell, sensitivity to magnetic fields and perfection of movement, what of its powers of vision? The actual structure of the eyes does not differ substantially from that of other vertebrates; but certain improvements have transformed them into astonishing instruments for gathering luminous information. The typically spherical shape of the vertebrate eye is slightly flattened sideways in sharks. Like the human eye, a shark's eye has a retina, a cornea, a lens, an iris and a pupil. A shark's retina, like the human retina, also has two types of cells, cones and rods, but sharks have a much higher percentage of the latter, developed for perceiving differences in light intensity, not of color. So there is a high degree of sensitivity to dim light and to moving objects. This does not imply that sharks see only in black and white; the fact that cones are present means that they have some perception of colors. The pupil, too, unlike that of the bony fishes, can dilate and contract, regulating light intensity. What is more, sharks possess a structure that assists their low-intensity vision: the *tapetum lucidum*, a layer of reflective cells also found in many mammals and birds with crepuscular and nocturnal habits, and which gives the eyes of such animals, including sharks, the aspect of tiny lighthouses when caught in a beam. The *tapetum lucidum*, located behind the retina, reflects some of the light initially released toward the sensitive cells in such a way that it can still be perceived and exploited for vision. In the same manner as bright light, therefore, it enables the species to see better. Apparently, the *tapetum lucidum* of sharks is twice as effective as that of cats.

The eyes of bony fishes (from top, a tropical mullet, a crocodilefish and a parrotfish) differ at first glance from those of sharks, which hunt mainly at night or toward dusk.

Another structure that distinguishes the eyes of some sharks from those of the bony fishes is known as the nictitating membrane because of its resemblance to that of birds; a shark can close this when the eyes are particularly endangered, as during the final stages of an attack on prey.

Although the average shark has good vision, there are a few

species with small or nearly non-functional eyes. These sharks are active at night and capture prey by using senses other than sight, such as hearing and electroreceptivity. The Squatinidae, for instance, possess small eyes and during the day live buried in the sand or mud. The whale sharks of the family Rhincodontidae and the megamouth species of the family Megachasmidae have no need of big eyes for catching the tiny prey they eat. But the thresher sharks of the family Alopiidae and the crocodile shark, *Pseudocarcharias kamoharai*, possess enormous eyes, suggesting that they hunt actively at dusk and even at night.

Hearing and Feeling

Considering that many oceans, especially those of high productivity, provide poor underwater visibility, sight is a sense that is employed only as a backup after hearing and

Nocturnal predators, the tawny nurse sharks, *Nebrius ferrugineus, of the Indo-Pacific rely mostly on their sense of smell to locate and identify their prey.*

smell have successfully registered the presence of prey at an indeterminate distance. Several experiments have confirmed that the vision of sharks is effective at a distance of about 15 m (50 ft).

The auditory sense first alerts the hunter that there may be something in the vicinity worth eating. Like other nonterrestrial animals, sharks do not have a direct link between the hearing mechanism and the outside world, but only an inner ear. This is formed of three chambers turned in three directions, and a fourth that contains an otolith, resembling a small stone, which determines the shark's direction and orientation. Because the passage of the sounds is indirect, perhaps through the skeletal cartilage, sharks can pick up only low frequencies, from 25 to 100 Hz; these are the same low frequencies emitted by animals that are dying or struggling after being hooked or shot by a fisherman. This is why sharks arrive so promptly after a skin-diver has caught a prey. Some sharks can hear sounds at a distance of 250 m (800 ft).

Another sensory organ, complex and not fully understood, is the lateral line. As in bony fishes, sharks possess a long row of sensors that, starting at the head, surrounds the eyes and extends to the root of the first caudal fin; this constitutes the lateral line, a series of canals filled with fluid, which open to the outside through tiny pores. Inside the canals are cilia-like projections of sense cells, the neuromasts, which are particularly sensitive to water movements caused by turbulence, currents and vibrations. As in hearing, the lateral line is receptive above all to vibrations of low intensity, and enables the shark to take note of the slightest movements of the water and directional currents.

My First White Shark

by Valerie Taylor

I remember my first great white shark. It was Memory Cove, South Australia, 1968. She was attached to a shark fisherman's float, a huge steel hook through her lip. The shark was swimming in circles, very much alive.

At the time Ron was the only person in the world to have filmed a white shark underwater in its natural element. We still had not graduated to using a cage. Ron and I and our assistant were wondering how best to approach our find when a second great white some 5 meters in length suddenly appeared. Without hesitation the newcomer swam up and ripped open the trapped shark's stomach. Water boiled white, then red, a giant tail lashing the surface into pink foam.

We gaped in amazement. I thought, "I was about to jump in the water with that, I must be mad."

The attacker vanished as suddenly as he had appeared. Our hooked shark hung limp, her stomach torn open, her liver and heart devoured. It had all happened in less than two minutes. Two minutes of heart-stopping wild cannibalism between the most feared fish in the ocean and I was hooked for life.

Ron and I eventually entered the water to photograph the dead predator. I remember a prickly feeling, not fear but wariness, lest the killer return. I also remember the incredible awe almost reverence I felt as I ran my hands down the huge rock-hard head. The power of the beast had not diminished with death; her black eye seemed to watch me still, the triangle teeth ready to tear flesh.

During the following years we appeared in, or worked on, the feature films Blue Water White Death, Jaws, Jaws 2, Orca. *All featured a great white but the most memorable experience*

The Australian-born Valerie May Taylor, together with her husband, Ron, has for almost forty years been one of the most important and influential figures in the world of underwater exploration as revealed through book, photography and film. The documentary work done by the Taylors—pioneering and indeed revolutionary in content for its time—has been of inestimable value, notably in familiarizing the public with the behavior of sharks in general and the great white shark (*Carcharodon carcharias*) in particular. Indeed, it owes its status as a protected species largely to their dedicated public relations activities. Authors of many books, articles and documentaries, the Taylors have also made their work available to Hollywood, collaborating in the shooting of such films as *The Shark*.

The great white shark draws close to Valerie Taylor's stern platform.

I ever had did not occur while working on a fancy Hollywood production but one day when we were tucked up behind Little English Island in Spencer Gulf, South Australia, sheltering from rough weather.

A shark had been nosing around for some time. One of the crew started throwing out a fish on a line and pulling it away just as the shark went to take it, a type of teasing that usually sends the predator lunging about on the surface in a frustrated manner. We noticed almost immediately this shark reacted in a more subdued manner than was normal, calmly circling around ever closer to the charter boat's tiny swim platform. "See if you can bring her closer," said Ron, so I climbed down onto the platform, which was at water level, a fish in my hand. What followed was awesome. After several throws where the shark took the bait from my rope in a sweet and gentle manner, Ron suggested I hand-hold the fish and see what would happen. The white was swimming around a meter away, head just above the water, her matte black eyes watching. I offered her the fish. Without hesitation she swam to my feet and gently took the bait from my hand. I patted her head and offered more fish, all of which she took, piece by piece, daintily without haste.

We had an understanding, the shark and I. I felt secure, protected almost, it was a great privilege to be allowed such a rare gift. I can still feel the hard cold head beneath my hand, flesh connecting with flesh and the tingling surprise as I realized that the beast had in some primitive way accepted me. For a few minutes we lapsed into a state of harmony rarely experienced between wild predator and modern man. Although the fish was capable of rising above the water and snatching me from my rickety foothold, I knew I was safe. It was one of the most memorable few minutes of 45 years working in the ocean.

Fortunately Ron filmed the entire episode; otherwise I would feel reluctant to put such a strange experience into words.

The great white shark is next to man the ultimate predator—a superbly designed eating machine so perfect it has virtually not changed over 200 million years of evolution. It seems to know its place on the stage of life and it certainly knows how to put us in ours.

Ron and I continue to attract and study all shark species but the great white is the most difficult and elusive of them all. After 35 years of working with this most awesome of nature's creations, its private life is still a mystery and the desire to learn more an addiction that can never be quelled.

I am happy to say that Ron and I played a large part in having white sharks protected in Australian waters. Never numerous, they have been hunted to the brink of extinction. "Good" we may say "get rid of the brutes, we don't need sharks." Well, we don't need tigers either but isn't it nice to know that there is a place on this earth where this most magnificent of all creatures can still exist in the wild, roaming free and safe.

The huge predator approaches without any sign of fear and eventually seizes the fish offered by Valerie Taylor.

Thanks to their sophisticated system of propulsion, sharks appear to move without any effort through the water, even when confronted by the strongest currents.

FINS AND LOCOMOTION

Like Airplanes

The evolution of bony and cartilaginous fishes had a major impact on the development of the jaw. Previous vertebrates, the Agnathi, did not possess a true mouth with an upper and lower jaw, but simply a round hole enabling them to draw in prey from the bottom; and, as is the case with the modern lampreys, to suck at the organic tissues of the fish that they parasitized. The upper and lower jaw, and thus the ability to capture other species, therefore necessitated better control of the body than had formerly been possible. Hence, the first bony and cartilaginous fishes had to develop highly sophisticated external organs for the control of swimming: the fins. The primitive sharks usually possessed two dorsal fins, two pectoral and pelvic fins, and one caudal fin. The skeletal foundation of these fins consisted of a basic element from which extended long cartilaginous processes that ran almost to the tip of the fin. This structure did not allow for much movement of the fin itself, which functioned virtually on its own as a hydrodynamic wing, serving only to stabilize the body while swimming. The caudal fin of these sharks was also special. The notochord, which supported the body somewhat like a vertebral column, turned upward at the root of the tail, while the lower part was supported only by secondary elements; although from the outside the tail appeared symmetrical, this was not true of the inside.

New Fins in the Cretaceous

The second stage of adaptation occurred during the period from the Carboniferous to the Cretaceous and gave the Elasmobranchii the body structure they have today. In particular the fins began to take on their present-day form. Instead of a single large basic skeletal element, these sharks had three, together with other extensions that supported the structure. In this way the base of the fin itself was narrower, permitting freer movement. The internal muscles bent the fin in one direction or another. The swimming action gained immeasurably in speed and maneuverability. Above all it became possible, as is the case with modern sharks and many bony fishes, to vary the so-called angle of attack, namely the

angle at which the front part of the fin meets the water. The fins themselves, especially the pectorals, could therefore function as streamlined wings, assisting changes of direction and raising the snout of the shark while swimming. Thus, in present-day sharks the pectoral fins help to keep the body at a constant level. In the hammerhead shark species of the genus *Sphyrna*, the head, with its broad expansions on either side, is thought to function in much the same way. In many species the tail, too, changed form, becoming asymmetrical, with the upper lobe longer and stiffer than the lower lobe. Swimming became more swift and agile, facilitating pursuit of prey and flight from enemies.

Swimming in Modern Seas

Modern sharks, with the exception of the benthic species, tend to have two pectoral, two pelvic, two dorsal, one anal and one caudal fin, the last of which is the most important for propulsion and which in some forms takes on very specialized shapes. In the thresher shark, for example, the upper lobe is extremely long (equal to the rest of the body), while the lower lobe is shorter; these small, speedy animals use blows of the tail to stun the fishes they eat. The pelagic sharks that live on the high seas

Almost all Rajiformes, such as the eagle rays in the photograph, move through the water by flapping their pectoral fins like wings.

Sharks, such as this silvertip shark, Carcharhinus albimarginatus, *propel themselves mainly with the tail; on the other hand, the Rajiformes, such as the mantas, use their pectoral fins to provide the thrust.*

need to have stamina and be capable of sudden spurts of speed. The form of their tail is therefore similar to that of tuna and other swift ocean swimmers. They do not need a structure that provides agility because they are not compelled to carry out sudden braking or acceleration. The dorsal fins have the important job of stabilizing movement that might otherwise go into a roll that would compromise swimming. Some pelagic species that swim rapidly also have a small keel at the base of the tail that reduces turbulence when in motion.

The Problem of Keeping Afloat

No animal could survive if it had to swim continuously to keep afloat. Bony fishes have developed a special structure known as the swim bladder; filled with gas, it counterbalances gravitational pull that would cause them to sink. Sharks have a different structure, but with the same functions. The liver is filled with fatty acids and oils (particularly squalene). These compounds are less dense than water and thus make it possible for the shark to float. Above all, the species that live on the high seas and swim continuously have a large liver; that of the blue shark, *Prionace glauca,* weighs about one-fifth of the entire body weight. The counterbalancing action of the liver is so effective that a tiger shark of 4 m (13 ft), weighing almost 50 kg (120 lbs) in the air, weighs a mere 3.5 kg (7.5 lbs) in its element.

The cartilaginous skeleton likewise seems to have evolved to improve the floating capacity; cartilage, in fact, is lighter and more elastic than bone. Although it has been regarded, in evolutionary terms, as a less advanced tissue than bone, many scientists think that cartilage is an invention that has enabled the sharks to remain virtually unchanged for millions of years. These adaptations designed for efficient swimming have appeared in different guises. The sharks inhabiting the ocean bed are slow and lazy swimmers, hunting prey given predominantly to sudden bursts of speed. Their pectoral fins are often as broad as wings, comparable to those of skates and rays. The pelagic species, on the other hand, have long, slim pectorals, invaluable for rapid, continuous swimming.

The speed of sharks varies according to their lifestyle; it ranges from a few kilometers an hour for the whale and basking sharks to the 35 kmh (22 mph) bursts of speed of the shortfin mako.

GILLS AND RESPIRATION

Complex Mechanisms

One of the most evident external differences between the bony and cartilaginous fishes is the covering of the gills. The breathing apparatus of animals that live in the water, in fact, has to be in constant contact with the water to extract from it all the necessary oxygen. Both vertebrates and invertebrates are therefore provided with structures that are generally known as gills, even

The open gill slits of a tiger shark (left) compared with three examples (below) of gills protected by an operculum, characteristic of bony fishes such as the queen angelfish, Forster's hawkfish and a leopard grouper.

GILLS AND RESPIRATION

39

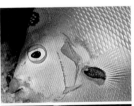

though they originate in diverse ways. The gills of sharks are highly vascularized plates, literally flushed with blood, positioned on broad arches of cartilage. Sea water passes from the mouth over the gill filaments that extract the oxygen from it. At the same time, just like the lungs of land vertebrates, the gills expel into the water the excess of carbon dioxide present in the blood. There are from five to seven gill openings or slits, and usually the more primitive families have a larger number. Each of them is covered with a flap of skin that protects the delicate structures. If the shark is a good swimmer, it is easy for the water to pass over the gills. In such cases the body movement itself forces the water to run over the gills, where the oxygen can be removed. It is a mechanism described as "jet ventilation," and it is adopted above all by the deep-sea predators such as the mako and the white shark. It is this very detail of behavior that has spread the legend that all sharks need to swim in order to breathe. Whereas this may be true of the pelagic species, others have a different system that enables them to rest on the sea floor without any problems. The water, in fact, is forced through the gills by an active mechanism defined as pumping; the entry and exit valves of the respiratory system are opened or closed, forcing the water that has entered the mouth

Contrary to what is believed, not all sharks need to swim continuously in order to breathe. Whitetip reef sharks, Triaenodon obesus, *often remain for long periods on the bottom.*

to flow out of the gills and release its oxygen content.

The metabolism of sharks is in fact closely linked to this oxygen content. Like almost all bony fishes, cartilaginous fishes are regarded as "cold-blooded"—a definition that is much employed but incorrect, for strictly speaking their blood is of variable temperature and they are scientifically known as ectotherms, meaning that they obtain much of their body heat from the outside. Most sharks come into this category, for their metabolism is fairly slow, not generating sufficient heat to maintain the body at a higher temperature than the surroundings. A few of them, however, are also endotherms, with a constant body temperature and capable of generating heat within the body by metabolism and other methods. The species that make up the family Lamnidae, for example, are endowed with a special set of structures and adaptations that enable them to retain a constant temperature, at least in certain parts of the body. One of the most interesting structures, in this context, is the so-called *rete mirabilis*, a very dense network of small arteries and veins, situated close to the "warm structures" of the body. In the white shark there is one network behind the eyes, which heats the brain, one over the liver for the intestines, and one surrounding the muscles. The *rete* functions as an exchanger of counter-current heat; when the warm, deoxygenated blood (deriving from the body) passes through the *rete* on its way to the gills, it transfers the heat to the arteries that run from the gills carrying the cold, oxygenated blood. Not too much of the heat thus exchanged is lost to the outside, and the shark remains warmer than its environment. The stomach temperature of the white shark, for example, is always around 25°C (77°F), independent of the water temperature. Such a high temperature enables the Lamnidae (to which perhaps may be added the thresher sharks) to be efficient predators and physiologically better developed than other fishes. The orbital network behind the eye sharpens the vision and increases neural activity by heating the eyes and the brain. The muscles, too, work better at the high temperature brought about by the *rete mirabilis*. And a further consequence is an improvement in digestive efficiency; the white shark feeds on marine mammals, whose bodies are often literally lined with fat, rich in energy but hard to digest. A speedier and more effective digestive process allows the shark to assimilate more rapidly the tissues on which it feeds.

Regional endothermy (the capacity to raise the temperature of only certain body zones), combined with a high value of hematocrit—the ratio, by volume, of red blood cells to whole blood— and hemoglobin, have led some to believe that the white shark and other fast-moving and active species have a very high rate of metabolism, at least in comparison with other sharks: metabolic values, in fact, to be compared with those of mammals. The obvious conclusion is that the body and blood supply of these animals are constant in temperature, just like mammals and birds, although conclusive proof has not yet been found. From the evolutionary and ecological viewpoint, high temperature and metabolism have enabled the white shark and other Lamnidae to live as well in cold zones, such as temperate and possibly even polar waters, meanwhile remaining active and aggressive predators. So, thanks to these evolutionary innovations, they have become the equivalent of lions and tigers of the ocean.

A researcher from the University of Miami accompanies a tiger shark in a semi-comatose condition, supplying oxygen to its gills so that it can resume swimming under its own steam.

TEETH AND PREDATION

Perfect Instruments

Although many characteristics of sharks may cause astonishment and inspire fear, one particular feature is unique to this subclass: the teeth. Evolved directly from the scales that cover the shark's body, the teeth are exquisite instruments for grasping, cutting, ripping and chopping, and they are subject to none of the defects that affects the teeth of mammals.

In structure they are very simple, for they are made of a nucleus of dentine covered with enamel, without a proper root. The enamel itself is constituted largely of apatite, or more precisely fluor-apatite (calcium phosphate) crystals; in the uppermost layer the crystals are arranged randomly to disperse the stresses caused by powerful bites. Since there is no root, each tooth is attached in a fairly loose manner to the jaw structure. For this reason, and also because of the violence of the bite, in some species the teeth come away quite easily from the membrane linking them to the jaws (the dental bed, made up of nonmineralized fibers). But this fact is compensated by a more brilliant evolutionary invention of the elasmobranchs; namely, the continual production of the teeth, which

Sharks possess teeth of extraordinary variability but all are equally effective. These pictures show the difference between the multiple rows of triangular teeth of an unidentified gray shark of the genus Carcharhinus (top) and the typically heart-shaped teeth of the tiger shark, Galeocerdo cuvier (bottom).

become, so to speak, infinite. The teeth are arranged in parallel rows, one behind the other, and the membrane covering the jaws moves forward so that the back teeth replace the ones in front as they fall out or are damaged. During their lifetime some sharks may replace up to 30,000 teeth. Under ideal conditions a young lemon shark, *Negaprion brevirostris*, may substitute all the teeth in its upper jaw every 8.2 days and that of the lower jaw every 7.8 days.

Obviously, the teeth of sharks are not all the same. The more than 400 species that populate the world's seas have evolved a series of adaptations for hunting which have transformed their dental structure. The smaller and faster sharks, which feed principally on mollusks such as octopus and squid, have long, pointed teeth, suitable for grasping slippery and elusive prey. The big species such as the white shark, which consume large adult prey such as sea lions, seals and large fishes, have triangular teeth

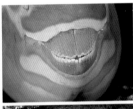

with a sawlike edge, whereby the victim's flesh is literally torn to shreds. The nurse sharks, which feed on benthic mollusks, have huge cone-shaped teeth that crack the thick shells of the prey. The Heterodontidae sharks possess two types of teeth: the front ones seize prey (sea urchins, starfish, crabs, shrimps) and the back ones split open the hard protective shell. The most highly modified teeth appear in the plankton-feeding species, such as the whale shark, the basking shark and the meg-

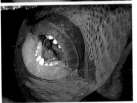

amouth, whose well-developed teeth have become tiny and hook-shaped, but have not vanished like those of the whalebone cetaceans (baleen whales and rorquals). The minuscule prey are sieved by the denticles and also by the very spacious gills.

A Sudden Attack

The techniques of hunting and capturing prey also vary considerably from species to species; the most interesting and unusual are those of the huge carnivorous sharks of the ocean, such as the white shark and the tiger shark. Having identified their potential prey with their remarkably keen sense organs, many sharks approach and simply swallow with a single gulp the fish or squid that has been targeted. Often, when the prey is not known, some sharks make a cautious approach to test out its "palatability." Not all sharks, in fact,

Several examples of the different types of specialized teeth of bony fishes: the fused beaklike dentition of the Scaridae (parrotfish), the strong teeth of the Balistidae (triggerfish), and the sharp fangs of a moray eel, a lizardfish and a barracuda.

The presence of an overdose of predatory stimuli frequently produces the phenomenon known as "feeding frenzy," during which sharks may turn dangerous.

Facing page: the spectacular teeth of the Caribbean reef shark, Carcharhinus perezi, *as it is fed by a skin-diver and photographed during a shark dive at Freeport in the Bahamas.*

simply sweep the seas clean, catching anything they can find; but the tiger shark, *Galeocerdo cuvier*, undoubtedly does, feeding on everything it comes across, from sea birds to turtles. Other species are far more selective. The weasel sharks (Hemigaleidae) feed almost exclusively on cephalopods whereas the *Mustelus* sharks consume crabs and crayfish. This is why the white shark sometimes bites a human, even quite violently, and then abandons its victim, considering it inedible. There have been instances, too, of sea birds having been seized by a shark as they alight on the surface, and being spat out virtually unharmed, being regarded as an unsuitable meal.

When the shark judges the prey appropriate, particularly when it is a large animal, the highly developed and complex biting mechanism comes into play. In contrast to many primitive shark species, the jaw of modern sharks is short and joined by elastic ligaments, at two points only, to the neurocranium. The shortening of the upper and lower jaws makes it possible for the shark to bite and grasp even a large victim and to tear off strips of flesh. When a requiem shark (family Carcharhinidae) approaches prey, its head draws back to expose the lower jaw. As the shark bites down on its victim, the entire jaw structure is simultaneously thrust forward. Precise calculations have shown that the bite of this shark exerts a force of two to three tonnes per square centimeter. The upper and lower teeth of the great white shark function exactly like a saw in stripping away pieces of flesh. The cutting power of the teeth enables it to rip off lumps of flesh even larger than the capacity of the jaws. Consequently, the shark will tackle animals as big as a whale, which is normally safe from hunters by virtue of its size.

Other families have adopted a variety of methods to capture prey. The strangest, perhaps, is that of the nurse sharks (Ginglymostomatidae), which have large fleshy lips and a muscular pharynx. Plunging these lips into fissures of rock, the sharks inhale water vigorously, creating sufficient pressure to suck prey into their mouth. The thresher sharks (Alopiidae) have a tail with a very long upper lobe, as long as

Two turtles, Chelonia mydas, *and* Eretmochelys imbricata, *having survived the attack of a tiger shark, bear visible signs of the predator's terrible teeth marks.*

Below: the sad and unnecessary death of a hammerhead caught in the course of a game-fishing expedition.

their body, which they use as a kind of whip to terrify fish and possibly to strike and stun them. The saw sharks (*Pristiophorus*), which possess a long snout edged with sharp teeth, invade shoals of fish and strike out at them with the rostrum before seizing them.

Probably the most astonishing method of feeding, however, is that of the cookiecutter shark, *Isistius brasiliensis*, which, although it is no more than 50 cm (20 in) long, is endowed with an enormously strong circular mouth with sharp teeth and will launch attacks on much bigger animals such as whales, other sharks, tuna and dolphins. It then proceeds to scoop out circular chunks of flesh from the victim's body, leaving all too visible scars on these giants of the ocean.

Sharks as Prey

Although, from an ecological point of view, sharks, particularly the large ones, are superpredators and very few are likely to be harmed by other carnivores, several of them, to avoid being captured, have had to adopt highly sophisticated defensive methods that may be either physical or behavioral. Some sharks of the family Heterodontidae, for instance, possess spines on the dorsal and anal fins that prevent a carnivore taking hold. The majority of sharks, however, rely on camouflage and a body appearance that blends with the sea floor. The sharks of the family Squatinidae, the angelsharks, and the wobbegongs, carpetsharks of the Australian family Orectolobidae, are perfectly mimetic. The latter tend to bite humans, not because they are particularly aggressive or dangerous, but because they spend the day lying on the bottom and a skin-diver may accidentally tread on them and trigger a reaction.

Some sharks keep well beyond the reach of their predators, living in the great depths of the ocean, whereas others grow to such an enormous size that they cannot be caught. These

are the species, like the whale shark, the basking shark and the megamouth, which feed on small and tiny animals such as pelagic shrimps or minuscule fish that congregate in shoals. In evolutionary terms, large dimensions imply a prominent position in the food chain, and hence little need for self-defense against predators. These species have an immense food reserve at their disposal because shrimps and shoaling fish feed on planktonic algae that draw energy directly from the primary source of life, solar rays. Because every stage of the food chain—from the sun's rays to plants, from these to herbivores and finally to carnivores—involves some loss of energy, animals that feed on shrimps and plant-eating fishes (present in vast numbers because they can draw on such an immense source of energy) are likely to grow prodigiously, so that a whale shark, for example, may measure 9–10 m (30–33 ft) in length.

Defence and Territory

Long regarded as primitive and unintelligent animals, sharks are in fact capable of complex and interesting modes of behavior. When it comes to defending themselves or their territory, certain sharks, especially the gray reef sharks, *Carcharhinus amblyrhynchos*, exhibit behavior patterns as elaborate as those of land vertebrates. Some of these maneuvers have been mistaken for deliberate attacks on humans, even though the danger is not immediate. One characteristic that shark behavior has in common with that of so-called superior animals is exaggeration of movement. When one shark approaches another with a view to expelling it from its territory, it swims with slow, ostentatious movements to underline its presence and the size of its body. The body is arched, the pectoral fins are lowered and the head is lifted. Very soon the lateral movements become spasmodic and the shark raises its snout and grinds its teeth. If the intruder does not turn tail, the shark may suddenly launch an attack and seriously injure its rival.

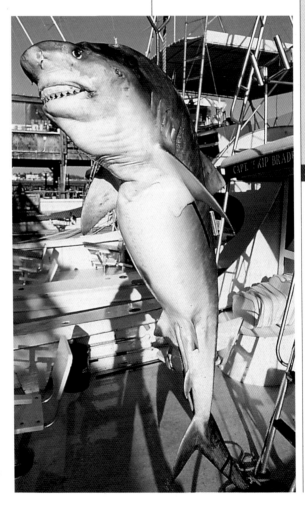

The grotesque sight of a large tiger shark, victim of big-game fishermen, and bearing the visible marks of high-caliber bullets, is displayed for the admiration of passersby.

Things Change

by Howard Hall

Today, sport divers travel to all corners of the globe searching for exciting encounters with sharks. The greatest of ocean predators are now featured attractions for live-aboard dive boats and sport diving resorts. Advertisements beckon customers with promises of waters filled with sharks. And divers flock to these destinations like fleas to the rump of a mangy dog. Twenty-five years ago this would have been considered madness.

Howard Hall is one of the world's most important underwater photographers and documentary filmmakers. Winner of six Emmy Awards for his documentaries, since 1970 he has made, together with his wife Michelle, sixteen episodes for the *Wild Kingdom* series, filmed several episodes for NOVA and Survival Anglia, the famous documentary *National Geographic Special: Sharks*, and three full-length features, including *Seasons in the Sea*, which won the prestigious Golden Panda Award.

His photographs and articles have appeared, among others, in *Life*, *National Geographic*, *Geo*, *Terre Sauvage*, *UWF* and *Airone*. He is also the author of various books, including *Howard Hall's Guide to Successful Underwater Photography*, *Sharks*, *The Kelp Forest*, and *Dolphins*.

There was a time, not so long ago, when the word "shark" struck fear in the hearts of even the most macho divers. Use of the word or images of these creatures was strictly taboo in dive magazines. Even the implication that sharks might be found in the waters frequented by vacationing divers would have been the death knell for a sport diving resort. When the movie JAWS was released, many dive shops and resorts saw a 40 percent drop in business. Sharks were not big business; they were bad business. No one wanted to see a shark underwater because we all knew that an encounter would almost certainly be followed by dismemberment and death. Those of us who continued to dive, during those dark times, were heroes indeed.

I preface this story with the above in hopes of, at least partially, explaining my own sniveling cowardice and stupidity in the story that follows.

My first encounter with a shark almost scared me to death. The year was 1971 and I was spearfishing more than a mile off the coast of La Jolla, California. For several hours I had been free-diving to forty or fifty feet and waiting silently in hopes that an eighty-pound white sea bass would swim within range of my six-foot-long speargun. With each dive, I imagined

The final phase of the attack of a blue shark, Prionace glauca—like that described by Howard Hall—on a mackerel, Scomber japonicus.

myself returning to the beach at La Jolla Cove and carrying my prize across the green park lawn to my car as beautiful women rushed to my side begging me to tell the story of my heroic adventure. This dream never quite came true. The largest white sea bass I ever managed to land was less than forty pounds. And the sight of a wet skin-diver flopping across the lawn covered with slime and fish blood never seemed to attract much positive attention from lovely women. On this particular morning, even a small white sea bass was not in the cards.

Not wanting to return to the beach without dinner, I shot a pair of small barracuda. These I attached to a fish stringer that I clipped to my weight belt in such a way that the dead fish flopped against my legs as I swam. Thus adorned, I began my mile-long swim back to the beach, leaving behind a trail of blood, scales and fish slime that could not have been more provocative to a passing shark than a sign painted on my butt that read "eat here." Now, you're probably thinking that only an idiot would swim a mile offshore with dead fish tied to his legs. But, ah . . . Well, you see, ah . . .

Anyway, I had made it back to within a few hundred yards of shore when I felt something large smack into the back of my

Highly aggressive predators, blue sharks are nevertheless also furnished with modified gill arches that serve to catch the minuscule planktonic organisms populating the high seas.

legs. Most people would have instantly soiled their Speedos if they felt something large smack into their legs while swimming offshore in a cloud of fish blood. But not I. I knew immediately what had hit me and I refused to show even the slightest trace of fear. It was obvious. Flip Nicklin, or one of my other spearfishing buddies, had expended great effort to sneak up on me to whack me with their speargun in hopes of causing my heart to explode. I was not going to give Flip the satisfaction. I casually bent down to look below and behind me. My forehead almost collided with the dorsal fin of a shark.

What happened next was the result of instinct, a circulatory system flooded with adrenaline, and a lack of anything better to do. The shark passed beneath me, descended ten feet, and then turned to make another pass. I moved the tip of my speargun eight inches to the left and the shark ran right into the sharp tip.

For a few brief moments, the shark struggled against the tip of my speargun. Then he pulled free and swam away, trailing a green plume of blood from the small wound in his head. I made a mad dash for the beach, constantly checking behind me in case the shark returned. A lesser man (or more intelligent one) would have discarded his catch. Not I. My blood saturated with adrenaline, I was determined to return to the beach, return from the very jaws of death, return with my catch intact, to be worshiped as a hero by the maidens ashore.

As I climbed up on the slippery rocks, the adrenaline drained from my system. Instead of marching triumphantly to my van with my catch thrown casually over my shoulder and carrying my trusty gun in the crook of my arm, I found my shaking legs wouldn't support me. For fifteen minutes I was helpless. I could do nothing but sit awkwardly on the wet rocks in a pathetic puddle of fish slime.

In 1971 I didn't know blue sharks from white sharks. All I knew was that if it was big and shaped like a shark, you were going to die. At first, I thought the shark that had attacked me was probably a ten-foot blue shark. A few weeks later, I revised my memory to accommodate a fifteen-foot great white. Years later, after decades of photographing sharks, I realize that the shark that tried to eat the fish attached to my fish stringer had certainly been a blue and probably no more than eight feet long. But in 1971, the animal had seemed a monster. Today sport divers routinely travel to shark-infested destinations where they pay to pet sharks larger and more ferocious than the blue. It is truly amazing how much things have changed.

Inhabitants of temperate seas, blue sharks are surely among the most handsome of the numerous shark species. Common in the Mediterranean, under certain excitable conditions they may pose a danger to humans.

Apparently smooth, the skin of sharks and rays is in fact surprisingly rough to the touch. It is actually composed of very large numbers of dermal denticles, unlike that of bony fishes (right, from top, that of the family Scaridae, of Antennariidae and of Sphyraenidae), which is covered with more or less overlapping bony scales.

The extraordinary hydrodynamic quality of sharks results partly from the particular structure of the skin. Facing page, from top: detail of the placoid scales of a Greenland shark, Somniosus microcephalus; of the nurse shark, Ginglymostoma cirratum; and of the ornamentation of a whale shark, Rhincodon typus.

SKIN

A Sophisticated Structure

The epitome of efficiency, stamina and speed, some sharks, with their streamlined body shape and remarkably powerful muscles, are perfect swimmers. Yet they owe part of their predatory success to the intricate and specialized nature of their skin. Unlike the scales of fish, which in most species tend to be broad and flat, the placoid scales (or dermal denticles) of sharks are pointed. Each scale has a basal plate, a pedicel and a crown that encloses it. On the outside it is covered with enamel and dentine, and there is a central pulp cavity that contains a nerve and blood vessels. The resemblance to real teeth is obvious, and students of shark evolution are in fact convinced that the teeth themselves are simply modified scales; like the teeth, the denticles vary from one species to another and are often useful in identifying a particular species. In contrast to the scales of bony fishes, however, the placoid scales of sharks do not grow in concentric circles, following the growth of the animal itself; as the shark gets older, in fact, the number of scales simply increases. This means it is not possible to calculate the age of the animal from the size of its scales.

In the course of evolution, the placoid scales have been modified to perform other functions. In one family of sharks (Rhinobatidae) there is a series of small, sturdy projections along the back. The Heterodontidae, however, have proper spines close to the dorsal fins. Both these structures are modified scales and are clearly designed to ward off predators.

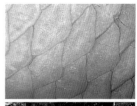

The arrangement of the scales or denticles nevertheless conforms to precise principles that serve to perfect the swimming action. It may seem a paradox that the skin of sharks is so rough: detailed experiments, however, have shown that if the skin surface was smooth, the water flowing over the body would produce vortices and countercurrents—forms of water turbulence that would slow down swimming. The individual scales break up these currents and thus permit a more speedy and efficient swimming action. This theory has also demonstrated the fact that the pelagic sharks, the strongest swimmers, have smaller scales than the benthic forms and that small scales are better than big ones in breaking up the water currents.

The rough skin of sharks has its commercial uses: the dressed skin of certain species was once used like sandpaper, especially by shipbuilders who needed a perfectly smooth surface.

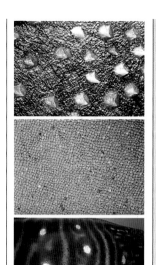

Colors and Shapes

The skin of sharks, perfected by long evolution, is capable of responding as well to other needs, peculiar to individual families. Apart from modification of the scales, the skin may change its color, consistency, strength and thickness. One of the most variable factors is coloration. The inactive, mimetic species that live on the seabed, such as the carpetsharks (Orectolobidae) and angelsharks (Squatinidae), in addition to long appendages resembling algae, have a marbled skin pattern that camouflages them against the bottom, from where they can launch attacks on passing prey without first alerting them to their presence. The pelagic species, on the other hand, are all more or less light on the belly and dark on the back. This type of coloring, described as countershading, prevents the prey from identifying the shark

A female gray reef shark,
Carcharhinus amblyrhynchos,
*exhibits a number of wounds
following an over-violent
courtship. For this reason, the
skin of the females is much
thicker than that of the males.*

*Right: an oceanic whitetip
shark,* Carcharhinus longimanus, *accompanied by ever-
present pilotfish,* Naucrates
ductor. *Below: a group of
remoras cluster in the cloaca
of a female whale shark,*
Rhincodon typus.

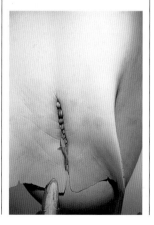

from below, since the pale belly seen from underneath blends with the tone of the sea surface. The dark back, by contrast, enables the predator to lie in ambush, as does the great white shark in the neighborhood of seal or sea lion colonies, resting on the bottom without being observed and launching an attack when the prey least expects it.

In the tiger shark, *Galeocerdo cuvier*, the zebra shark, *Stegostoma fasciatum*, and other species, the coloration of the young differs from that of the adults, probably because their colors (with large black and white patches, reproducing those of the seabed struck by sunlight) conceal them from predators. The adults, however, have no such need and their coloration is more uniform. Some sharks that inhabit deep water, such as the small, strange cookiecutter shark, *Isistius brasiliensis*, have a luminous skin, although its function is still not understood; it may prove useful to disorient predators or it may have something to do with communication between individuals.

Friends and Foes

The thickness of the skin likewise varies, according to conditions, species and sex. Because shark courtship includes some rough moments, the skin of the females is thicker than that of the males, to withstand the latter's bites.

Despite the strong skin and surface denticles, sharks, like other animals, are affected by external parasites. The most celebrated, which are better defined as commensals than parasites, are the remoras or suckerfish. Their dorsal fin is greatly modified, almost transformed into an adhesive organ. Attaching themselves to sharks, but also to whales, manta rays and other large fish, remoras travel the oceans without expending much energy and benefit from the remains of meals; or at least that is what was thought until quite recently. What really seems to happen is that the remoras grasp the sharks only when the latter change direction, while for the rest of the time they ride the waves in their wake (just like pilotfish, which certainly do not guide sharks, as was formerly believed). Moreover, the remoras are of value to their hosts as they consume the parasites that infest their skin; the stomach contents of some remora species, in fact, are made up almost entirely of copepods that attack the skin of sharks. These parasites take hold of the rough skin of the shark and feed on the tissues of the host, probably without causing

The skin of sharks is often infested by irritating parasitic copepods of the genus Dinemura, as in the case (left) of the mako. Below: a scalloped hammerhead, Sphyrna lewini, *is subjected, in this spectacular shot, to the attentions of a butterflyfish at a "cleaning station."*

them much harm but general irritation. Other parasites take up position in various places, including the most irritating, such as the cloaca or even the corneas of the eyes; this is the case with *Ommatokoita elongata*, which lives attached to the Greenland shark. It would seem, too, that this species is bioluminescent and can in some way attract prey toward the shark itself.

All these external parasites are a nuisance to the shark but for other animals they may be a source of food. As happens with many species of bony fish, sharks, too, especially those that live close to the bottom and are more subject to the attacks of parasites, frequent "cleaning stations." Here, tiny shrimps and fish specialized in catching parasites boldly approach the predators and begin the delicate work of removing the parasites. In this manner they eat and at the same time rid the shark of its irritant; indirectly, too, they offer opportunities to photographers who can take advantage of their subject's inactivity to get in for a close-up.

A Strange Place to Live
The excretory metabolism of sharks is rather special, for it

uses urea to establish an osmotic balance between the cells and the surrounding water. Thus, the water around a shark's body is likely an inhospitable area, since few animals can withstand such a strong poison. Only one group of platyhelminthes, the flatworms, have evolved metabolic mechanisms for defense against urea. So far, some 400 species of platyhelminthes have been classified, living as internal parasites of sharks.

Many bony fishes take advantage of the pressure waves generated by the swimming action of large sharks to expend less energy. Above: golden trevallys, Gnathanodon speciosus, *"riding" a whale shark; right: several* Elagatis bipinnulata *accompanying a silvertip shark,* Carcharhinus albimarginatus, *in the Andaman Sea.*

REPRODUCTION

Love's Labour

As we have already seen, the subclass Elasmobranchii is far removed from the popular image, cultivated in former years, of stupid predators. So it is not surprising that in one particular aspect of behavior, that of reproduction, shark evolution is almost on a par with that of the higher vertebrates.

Comparatively little is known of the courtship and mating rituals of the majority of sharks, considering that they often occur at night and in deep, secluded places. Analysis of their structure suggests that among the smaller, more flexible species, the male wraps his body during copulation around that of the female. In the bigger, more cumbersome species, however, the two sexes position themselves side by side. In order to keep his grip on the female, the male often bites his partner's pectoral fins or her back. Although as a safeguard the female has thicker skin, there is often visible evidence of the numerous scars left by his bites.

Fertilization is always internal, because the male penetrates the female with either of two claspers (pterygopodia), long organs derived from a modification of the pelvic fins. During copulation he extends the organ and inserts it into her cloaca. At this point a muscular pump expels the mass of spermatozoa along a canal in the pterygopodium into the female's body. Males of certain species have hooks on the clasper which attach to the walls of the female oviduct, ensuring that the mating act cannot suddenly be interrupted by another male.

Few but Viable

It is mainly in a series of evolutionary strategies that the elasmobranchs give proof of their advanced development. The majority of bony fishes lay thousands, even millions, of eggs that are scattered through the waters of seas, lakes and rivers. The reproductive effort of the females is directed entirely to the production of eggs, and after laying them, they do little to defend their young from consequent dangers. Thus, the bony fishes rely above all on luck and sheer numbers. Sharks employ a different strategy. Very few young are born, from one to a few dozen. Even the most prolific species give birth to no more than a hundred or so offspring.

This procedure uses up most of the female's energy in the production of eggs (which are large and full of yolk) and furthermore in the production of food for the tiny embryos, which are born directly from her body. So, it is true to say the sharks have evolved, independently of other animal groups, all the methods of egg development.

The oviparous species, such as the Port Jackson shark and the catshark, often choose a safe and well-protected site on the

57

An extraordinary sequence showing a female lemon shark, Negaprion brevirostris, *giving birth in shallow waters.* Below: the claspers (male sexual organs) of a smalleye hammerhead, Sphyrna tudes.

Many sharks, unlike that pictured on the preceding page, are oviparous. Above: a sequence showing the birth of a baby swell shark, Cephaloscyllium ventriosum, as it emerges from the egg.

sea floor to lay their eggs, which are enclosed in a kind of strong, horny theca or sheath. The mother takes care to deposit them in a place where they are rinsed by a constant current, for although the casing wards off danger, there is a risk of it depriving the embryo of the oxygen in the water which is indispensable for growth. The structure of the sheath, therefore, is such that the water that flows over it is channeled through tiny openings along its edge. Oxygen-rich water thus seeps in through the pores, and the water inside, from which the embryo has already extracted the precious gas, is expelled by the same route. The young grow at the expense of the yolk and are born fully developed and ready to go hunting.

Attentive Mothers

In other species, the egg is not expelled from the mother's body and birth occurs in a different way. About 70 percent of sharks are ovoviviparous, whereby the egg develops inside the mother, receiving little or no nutriment from her, or viviparous, whereby live young are born directly and are fed by the mother.

The former method of gestation is known as aplacental ovoviviparity. The eggs remain in the maternal uterus (or more precisely in the extended portion of the oviduct which functions as uterus), where they develop until the moment of birth when the baby sharks are born, independent and active, and capable of feeding. The mother merely affords them protection during the hazardous period of embryonic development but there is no connection between her body and the growing embryo.

A step forward is represented by other sharks in which the embryo is nourished with the yolk for a limited period. After that, the mother begins to feed the young with a special secretion, a kind of uterine milk that is available until the actual birth. This milk is ingested and absorbed by the developing embryo. This is called aplacental viviparity and it has recently been discovered that whale sharks come into this category, for a gravid female was found carrying some 300 uterine embryos, some of them still inside the egg, complete with yolk.

In the Lamnidae, the thresher sharks and other species, by contrast, the young are nourished on the eggs present in the maternal uterus; these eggs are unfertilized, about the size of a pea, and are available as food. The most extreme example of this growth process is to be found in the bull sharks; here the teeth of the babies in the mother's body are already visible, and the biggest of them start to feed on their siblings in the uterus. This is the only recorded instance of intrauterine cannibalism, although it is suspected that it may occur in other species as well. Thanks to this diet, the young shark may already measure as much as 1 m (3 ft) at birth.

Finally there are species that are decidedly viviparous, in

which a proper placenta is formed, not much different to that of mammals. When they begin to develop, these embryos likewise feed on yolk, but when this is finished, the vitelline sac is transformed into an umbilical cord attached to the mother's uterus. The young receive nourishment directly from the wall of the uterus through a highly vascularized structure that also carries away the waste products. Thus, the placenta is a mixture of maternal and embryonic tissues, exactly as in mammals. There are further strange similarities with mammals because, apart from internal fertilization, sharks possess the same reproductive hormones and the gestation period is of equal duration to that of certain land animals.

Perils of Birth

These reproductive strategies have both positive and negative implications. If just a few already grown young are born, no danger is posed in the course of egg development, and so the juvenile mortality rate is low. The fact, too, that the young are quite big at birth affords protection from predators, especially from other sharks. Yet this may itself be perilous for the population at large. The significance of slow development and the birth of only a few young is that commercial fishing, as widely practiced today, may threaten the very survival of some populations, if not of entire species. As happens with land mammals that develop slowly (gorillas and elephants in particular), many shark populations, once they begin to diminish, are slow to recover and run the risk of never getting their numbers back to a safe level.

Several shark species observe segregation of the sexes: many carcharhinids form sedentary groups of females at precise spots along a reef, while immature individuals (above) never stray far from nurseries in shallow water where they are best protected.

Problems of Coexistence

Sometimes, sharks eat humans. Much more often, humans eat sharks; or, at least, they kill them for the liver and skin, the cartilage and the corneas; or, worse still, they do it by accident or for sheer enjoyment.

Certainly, attacks on humans create a great sensation. Yet the truth lies in the statistics: this is an event that is actually very rare. According to facts provided by the *International Shark Attack File*, an American organization that gathers all the information on confirmed and unprovoked attacks throughout the world, from 1907 to the present day there have been only 1,848 documented cases of sharks attacking humans in all the seas worldwide. The term "unprovoked" attack is used to describe any aggressive act not brought about by human disturbance, apparently motivated not by defensive instinct on the animal's part, but by the deliberate intention to kill.

Above: the gruesome spectacle of the aborted progeny of a female hammerhead, caught just prior to giving birth. At least sixteen sharks have died at a single stroke. Below: the silhouette—similar to that of a sea lion—of a surfer seen from below, probably an explanation for various attacks on humans by white sharks.

60

The major culprit in such instances is certainly the great white shark, even though it is difficult to draw up a list of the other most aggressive sharks where humans are concerned, given that it is not easy to verify sightings and to identify the species in question. Among the more dangerous, however, are the tiger shark, certain of the Carcharhinidae (particularly the fearsome bull shark, *Carcharhinus leucas*), the lemon shark, the blue shark and the hammerheads. The majority of these species will generally launch an attack when disturbed; but only the white shark and the tiger shark will deliberately hunt humans. Again, though, it is not clear why they act like this: if in their eyes we simply represent a tasty snack, there would be few quiet and safe beaches anywhere in the world, and attacks would be much more frequent. Yet this is not the case. The likelihood is that only in exceptional circumstances will sharks be spurred into action that constitutes real danger for us. The *International Shark Attack File* comes up with a significant finding: it would appear that in U.S. waters the percentage of attacks on swimmers is decreasing whereas those on surfboarders are increasing in number. Researchers think that a surfer lying flat on a board and being propelled by his arms looks much more like something edible than a mere swimmer: his outline may be more easily confused, seen from below, with that of a seal or a sea lion, choice prey for

a white shark. This may explain the tendency of such sharks to attack people when they see them as prey to be devoured. In the Mediterranean, Italy has been the scene of most shark attacks, namely sixteen, of which seven have been fatal.

Who Is Threatening Whom?

If, on the one hand, we need to be wary of sharks and never underestimate their potential danger, we need to bear in mind that throughout the world's oceans, cartilaginous fishes such as rays, mantas and electric rays are being freely slaughtered. The killing is on a sufficient scale to threaten the survival of many species and perhaps prove a peril to the equilibrium of many marine environments in which sharks occupy the role of predators at the apex of the food chain.

Why do humans hunt sharks? Economic motives may have had some validity at one time when technology did not exist to re-create artificially the substances that cartilaginous fishes provided naturally. Apart, obviously, from their gastronomic value: many species have tasty flesh and are much in demand in many parts of the world, and their fins, moreover, are used in the Far East for the preparation of special dishes (though, ironically, on their own they are quite bland, for the taste comes wholly from the condiments employed). The major consumers, in fact, are our own domestic companions, cats and dogs: shark meat, either ground up or in chunks, is an ingredient of some pet foods. That said, it may also feature, unknown to the customer, as an ingredient of a fast-food "fishburger" or, under a different name (such as rock salmon) in a fish-and-chip shop: a risky procedure, considering that the tissues of the superpredatory shark may often contain large concentrations of mercury (and other toxic elements), scattered through the seas worldwide as a result of human industrial pollution.

Above: fins just cut off and ready to be dried, and preserved delicacies of shark's fins from China.

HOW YOUR SOUP IS MADE

Shark fins, the principal ingredient of a typical Chinese soup, are usually obtained by the barbarous practice of "finning." Sharks trapped in nets are hauled on board the trawler and there—alive and powerless—they are mutilated by the fishermen who cut off the tail and the fins with sharp knives. In this sad plight—and still living—they are thrown back into the water, condemned to sink to the bottom and to a protracted, agonizing death. Finning—denounced by many nations—nevertheless continues to be practiced, in the absence of any controls or sanctions.

A Cruel Trade

The use of shark skin, fortunately, is not as fashionable as it once was, except perhaps for turning out a souvenir item of doubtful taste. In the past, however, the skin was in keen demand for its abrasive quality, thanks to its strong denticles. Known commercially as "shagreen," it was used, prior to the arrival of sandpaper, by cabinet makers, carpenters and ivory

Making a detailed study of sharks is no easy task. Above: Guido Dingerkus takes a blood sample from a lemon shark to check on hormonal levels. Below: biologist Brad Wetherbee of the University of Hawaii ties an identification tag to a tiger shark that has been suitably sedated.

craftsmen. It was also used to make particularly handsome objects of furniture or to cover sword grips (especially the precious *katana* of Japanese samurai) to make the grasp firmer. Today it is still possible, especially in the United States, to buy cowboy belts and stirrups made out of shark skin: the stuff of folklore, perhaps, but a regrettable practice.

Shark's liver, rich in oils, has likewise been used over the centuries. In Australia, at one time, the extract served as fuel for lamps. But liver oil began to be exploited on a large scale when it was found to contain, among other constituents, large quantities of vitamin A and then when a Japanese scientist, in 1916, isolated a substance called squalene. This is still employed in many industries, including cosmetics and pharmaceuticals, as a base for beauty creams, drugs and ointments.

In medicine, parts of the shark are still used to cure various diseases. The corneas are an important raw material for human transplants, while certain polyunsaturated acids, again extracted from the liver, have found a use as an anticoagulant in the treatment of some serious forms of heart attack. The cartilage tissue is utilized as a culture base for generating skin for transplants in the case of major burns, while its use for fighting some forms of cancer is still controversial and yet to be proven.

Another important cause of mortality among sharks is game-fishing. This has been popular for many years and is promoted by specialist branches of the tourist trade, offering fishermen the thrilling experience of catching particularly combative species such as the fox shark, tiger shark and blue shark. Very often the victims of this "sport" are just killed and thrown back into the sea, merely satisfying the sense of capture.

Countless deaths of sharks and rays are caused accidentally by being caught up in the nets of trawlers, which practice highly profitable but environmentally damaging fishing methods. The use of such nets often entails a huge percentage of waste, up to 90 percent of the catch, judged useless from the commercial point of view.

Inevitably, sharks feature significantly in this enormous catalog of vulnerable marine animals. According to WWF estimates, between 30 and 70 million cartilaginous fishes are killed every year for their flesh, fins, skin and internal organs, providing the life-blood for an activity practiced by more than 120

of the world's nations and whose victims increased, during the five years 1990–1995 by 120 percent. At the same time, a growing demand and a corresponding rise in prices has been reported, in an upward spiral that bodes no good for the future of sharks.

In attempts to stem this senseless massacre, the governments of some countries, taking a cue from environmentalists, have begun to give serious thought to their fish resources, based on facts supplied by experts, who affirm that seas are becoming impoverished at an alarming rate. With a view to preventing the threatened exhaustion of marine resources, which would lead to a genuine economic catastrophe, a number of international agreements have been signed in recent years, with the intention of defining fishing zones and limits. Sharks, for their part, stand to benefit from such initiatives. The most important of these agreements was signed in October 1998 in Rome, under the aegis of the FAO, whereby the members of the United Nations were called upon to present, during 2001, fishing plans to guarantee the survival of shark species. Today, again under the flag of the United Nations, a global plan of action is under review whereby agreement will be sought on a common shark conservation policy to be adopted by all member nations.

Defining a common policy is in itself a difficult task, since it is hard to establish to what extent certain shark species are in danger of extinction. And the fact that the data is so indeterminate has given a number of nations the excuse to set no limits to the fishing of certain species. Others, such as South Africa and the United States, have redoubled their efforts for increased protection, yet these are off-the-cuff interventions, of doubtful efficacy, because each nation, according to the international fishery laws, has jurisdiction only over the waters within 200 miles of its coasts. Outside these limits there is total deregulation, and each country is free to do anything it wishes, even to hunt the rarest species, without risk of incurring any sanctions.

Two biologists from the University of Miami prepare to examine a blacktip shark, Carcharhinus limbatus, which will subsequently be released unharmed. Below: a gravid female lemon shark is followed across the breeding area of the Bahamas Banks.

My Fear for Sharks

by Marty Snyderman

It was three o'clock in the morning and we were 40 miles from the nearest point of land as we shone our lights down the line of floats that keep the top of the gill net near the surface. Six hours earlier we had seen a number of dorsal fins cutting across the surface of Mexico's Sea of Cortes as the fishermen we had joined stopped their skiff to set the net just before sunset. There was no question in their minds that the dorsal fins were those of scalloped hammerhead sharks and that they had a good chance for success in the coming night.

We had checked the net two hours earlier, but it was empty. This time things were different. Several of the floats had been pulled under, giving a good indication that there were sharks in the net. Of course, there is no way to know that the cause of the bobbing floats was not dorado, marlin, a sea lion, or even a whale that had become entangled. In fact, the previous day we had come across the remains of a Cuvier's beaked whale that was enveloped in a gill net that had been lost at sea.

Film producer, camera operator, photographer, author and lecturer from San Diego, California, Marty Snyderman is one of today's most prolific and influential authorities on life in the underwater world. Winner of an Emmy Award, he has directed and produced a number of documentaries on sharks for the *Nature* series for PBS, the National Geographic Society, the Discovery Channel and the Audubon Society. His articles and photographs have appeared in the *National Geographic Magazine, Audubon, Ocean Realm, Newsweek* and *Skin Diver.*

His publications are *California Marine Life, Shark: Endangered Predator of the Sea, The Living Ocean, Ocean Life, Guide to Marine Life of the Caribbean, Florida, and Bahamas,* and the CD-ROM *Sharks.*

I was working as the cinematographer on a television special that I was co-producing with my friend Rocky Strong, and there is no question that Rocky and I were excited about the dive. We were hoping to document one of the ways that sharks are exploited by humans and for the purposes of our film, we needed the fishermen to be successful.

No matter how experienced a diver you are, there is always a little anxiety when you roll over the side of your boat in the middle of nowhere in the middle of the night over water that is several thousand feet deep. Add the presence of a net and the likely possibility of encountering big sharks and you get a good idea of why there was an air of tension mixed in with our excitement.

A few minutes later Rocky and I, as well as our assistants Carlos Navarro and Russ Graham, found ourselves underwater swimming down the net. It always seems so odd to me that when I am on the boat prior to making a night dive in these conditions that I feel a knot in the pit of my stomach, but as soon as I am in the water away from the safety of the boat, I feel far more relaxed and the knot disappears. Shortly after we descended we could see the glow of a big hammerhead that was entangled in the net. Soon we saw three more hammerheads and two silky sharks.

No doubt about it, the night was very rewarding for the fishermen, and we would get the footage we had hoped for. But as I swam down the net I was haunted by images that danced in my head. Only a few months earlier I had watched a number of other scalloped hammerheads being cleaned, not by fishermen, but by barberfish, Spanish hogfish, and king angelfish as the sharks swam along the reefs at Costa Rica's Cocos Island. The seven- to eleven-foot-long sharks were a stunning sight. They appeared muscular, handsome and graceful all at the same instant as they approached the cleaning stations.

That day Mark Thurlow and I tucked ourselves in behind the rocks and waited in silence. We were diving closed-circuit rebreathers in an effort to get my movie camera close to

The horrifying sight of a group of scalloped hammerheads, Sphyrna lewini, *trapped on the seabed off Wolf Island in nets laid illegally in the Galapagos Marine Reserve. Thousands of sharks are pointlessly killed daily in the same way throughout the world.*

the cleaning stations. The sharks suddenly materialized out of the distant blue haze, swarmed over the reef, got cleaned, and then disappeared into the distance. So few people ever get to witness such a scene in nature. It seems to me to be the underwater equivalent of a wildebeest migration across an African plain or the gathering of great herds of caribou in Alaska. It is truly an awe-inspiring, yet very humbling, sight.

As I swam down the net that knot in my gut returned. It was a knot of fear, but clearly it was not a fear of the sharks, but fear for them. I suddenly felt a huge sense of responsibility that our film had to show our audiences what is happening to shark populations around the world. We have to encourage all nations to fish responsibly.

Not too many years ago the shark fishery in the Sea of Cortes was for local markets and restaurants. Today in Mexico and so many Third World nations, things are very different. Odds were that the sharks in the net would end up in Japan or in some other Asian country where they would be served up in a bowl of soup, used as an aphrodisiac, or sold for some scientifically unsubstantiated medicinal function. Global economics have greatly altered the fishery. In only a few hours these sharks would be finned, processed, and picked up by a refrigerated truck that would take the meat to Mexico City before it was shipped to the Orient.

I am not one to say that no one should ever eat a shark or any other fish. Certainly it is difficult to blame poor fishermen who are trying to feed their families. Their lives are demanding and very dangerous. But what gives me great

Exceptionally powerful and truly bizarre in appearance, hammerheads are very difficult to approach underwater; they seem to be especially bothered by divers' exhaust bubbles.

concern is that so many shark fisheries around the world are unregulated, and that in regulated shark fisheries, all too often, the regulations are not well enforced. The bottom line is that all too often our species is over-fishing shark populations. Many species are severely threatened, and in some cases the sharks have completely disappeared.

I have seen scalloped hammerheads and many other species of sharks in the wild, in all their glory. Those are moments I will always cherish. Too many times I have seen greatly threatened species of sharks being over-exploited by our species for short-term economic benefit. What a tragedy it is when scalloped hammerheads and so many other magnificent species of sharks are fished beyond their ability to replenish their populations. We know better, yet that is exactly what is happening all over the globe.

And that knot of fear in my gut just won't go away.

Immense shoals of hammerheads, comprising hundreds of individuals, offer skin-divers one of the most astonishing and memorable sights anywhere in the underwater world. Their habit of gathering together, however, renders them that much more vulnerable to fishermen.

From eighteenth-century engravings to the cover of one of the leading illustrated magazines of our time, the shark has invariably been portrayed as a monstrous, aggressive creature.

MYTHS AND LEGENDS

A Bogeyman for Modern Times

"Man-eater," "white death," "assassin" are just a few of the highly charged terms that have been applied to the shark, or more precisely, to the great white shark, which lately, and to its great misfortune, has become the archetype of them all in the popular imagination. Yet the image of the terrible predator, the mortal danger of the seas, and every swimmer's fearsome nightmare, has in fact been conjured up only recently. It was a series of incidents in Australian waters, dating from the 1960s, which successively claimed the lives of three champion skin-divers, that helped promote this psychotic conception of the killer of the seas. It was a phobia that found its ultimate expression in Peter Benchley's canny best-seller *Jaws*, published in 1974 and made into the enormously popular Steven Spielberg film in 1975. From that moment, sharks became the symbols of death lurking in the oceans; and it is surely no coincidence that Benchley himself later publicly made amends for the harmful image he had helped to foster by working actively for their welfare.

Until that time, matters had been quite different. Western civilization had given very little thought to marine predators. Interest, for what it was, centered more specifically on whales, as in Herman Melville's 1851 novel *Moby Dick*. And in any event, cetaceans had always played a positive rather than a negative role in popular imagination. As for sharks, there was no sign of them. The totemic animals of European culture were typically terrestrial and essentially rural: wolves and bears, above all.

Even so, sharks were well known. Aristotle, in one of his several treatises on zoology, *De Partibus Animalum*, gave detailed descriptions of their characteristics, showing that he had already identified, in the cartilaginous skeleton and gill openings uncovered by an operculum, the principal features of these fish. Other observations were less accurate: Aristotle maintained that sharks were compelled to turn on their back to bite their prey because of the ventral position of the mouth. This is incorrect; it may happen sometimes that a shark, confronted with a large prey will turn in the water on its own axis (as do crocodiles) in order to take a mouthful more easily, giving the impression of turning upside-down to deliver its bite. The great Greek philosopher also spoke of electric rays, showing that he was aware of their habit of stunning their prey with powerful shocks (today it has been verified that these are genuine electric shocks of more than 200 volts), and capable, too, of incapacitating humans. His observations imply that a seagoing civilization like ancient Greece must have been quite familiar with the ocean's animal life, including sharks.

For many centuries to come, apart from notes on nature by

Below: three illustrated plates from the Natural History of Fishes by Marcus Eliezer Bloch, published in Germany in the late eighteenth century. They show various recognizable shark species, correctly reproducing their essential features.

scientists and adventurers, there was scarcely a mention in Europe of sharks, not even in the context of myth and legend. Nevertheless, it is likely that certain shark species were at the origin of the numerous colorful descriptions of the fantastic marine monsters that roamed the pages of literature between the Middle Ages and the eighteenth century. The gigantic sea serpents, which many illustrations showed as crushing entire ships and crews in their coils, may well have been inspired by sightings of certain species.

Other strange discoveries of creatures similar to enormous marine reptiles, which occurred during the nineteenth century along the coasts of Scotland, were invariably the carcasses of basking sharks (*Cetorhinus maximus*) in advanced stages of decomposition; it has been demonstrated, in fact, that the detachment of the soft parts of these dead animals leaves carcasses that bear a surprising resemblance to the ancient plesiosaurs. And it was as an additional consequence of such findings that the legend of the Loch Ness monster, still in circulation today, found fresh momentum. The fossil teeth of sharks, especially the enormous tusks of *Carcharodon megalodon*, were mistaken for the tongues of dragons and petrified thunderbolts.

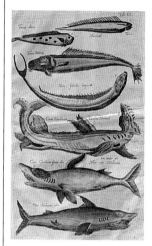

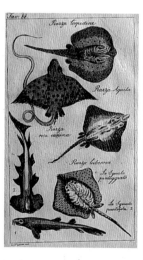

Gods of the Tropical Seas

Other civilizations outside Europe have developed even closer relationships with these extraordinary fish, often raising them to the status of divinity, and not necessarily with negative implications. The indigenous populations of the Pacific coasts of North America, for instance, often employed the motif of the shark in fashioning their totems. Sharks' teeth were used as arrowheads or substituted for the sharp blades of certain swords to make them even more deadly; such weapons were carried by some native tribes who used the teeth of the Greenland shark for this purpose.

The cultures in which the shark made, and still makes, its most frequent appearance, were those in the islands of the Pacific, in Oceania, Australia and New Guinea. Within this area, the sharpened teeth of sharks once served to create terrifying offensive weapons, such as swords and spears, while the tough skin formed an ideally strong covering for shields. In the Solomon Islands, species that were elsewhere feared as man-eaters were instead prized as valuable allies, capable of rescuing drowning swimmers and bringing them back to shore. Such services, however, were confined to fishermen who respected sharks and not to the forest dwellers who did not subscribe to these beliefs.

It was a common conviction in the Indo-Pacific that the most deserving of mortals would be reincarnated in the guise of the tiger shark, guardian and protector of their poorest relatives. Ancient ruins on the Polynesian islands testify to the cult of the shark-god, whose children and messengers are not only lovingly cared for in appropriate bathing pools excavated in the coral barrier reefs but also sometimes emerge at night from the billows, incarnated as sea messengers to be united with the children of the tribe; traces of the shark-god cult survive to this day in certain aspects of Polynesian culture.

The warlike Maoris of New Zealand have since distant times enjoyed a privileged relationship with the speedy mako shark, whose sharp teeth take on special symbolic meaning. For certain Australian Aborigines, the shark has importance not so much for its divine powers as for its economic worth: the large oily liver is tasty and much prized for its nutritive value.

In the Far East, one of the most exclusive and expensive delicacies is provided by sharks' fins, cooked in different ways, including the celebrated soup. These are traditional recipes, originating locally in coastal zones where sharks have always been accessible and affordable. Unfortunately, this has today become a really serious problem as what began

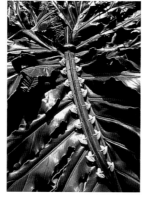

as local custom and economic necessity has spiraled out of control with the business boom associated with Oriental cuisine. Now, with easier commercial access to the Chinese market, the trade in sharks' fins has gone beyond national bounds and serves a flourishing international market including the Western nations. As a result, fishing for sharks has increased alarmingly, involving cruelty on an unimaginable scale as the animals are mutilated aboard the trawlers (see box, page 61) and consigned to a terrible, lingering death.

Above: a sword studded with the teeth of the tiger shark (Kiribati, Pacific Ocean) and a knife decorated with the skin of a ray (Tibet, 1700). Left: an encounter between a skin-diver and a manta ray swimming free in nature is a hopeful symbol of our future relationship with, and attitudes to, the innocent inhabitants of the ocean.

Photographing Sharks

by Doug Perrine

In the old days, part of the fun of photographing sharks was that most people, even most divers, believed that you were some type of daredevil, who daily risked being devoured by your subjects. Nowadays, more people realize that sharks feed on other sea life, and are not "continually athirst for human blood," but few are actually cognizant of the true difficulties involved in this demanding endeavor.

The first difficulty with shark photography is the same difficulty with all wildlife photography. Animals that have survived in the wild have done so because they have learned, among other things, to avoid large unfamiliar creatures. If humans are not unfamiliar, then they have learned to avoid humans in particular. The ones that are slow to absorb this lesson are quick to be eliminated.

The second problem with shark photography is the problem with all underwater photography: water makes a very poor lens to shoot through. It is full of suspended particles that scatter light. On land, the problem of avoidance is usually solved with long

Texan-born Doug Perrine is one of the most important of living underwater photographers. After a long and varied career—he served in the Peace Corps in the Far East and subsequently taught English and became a marine biologist and a skin-diving instructor—he is today a photographer and writer, and president of the Innerspace Visions photographic agency. His pictures have been published in dozens of books and hundreds of magazines throughout the world, including *National Geographic, Newsweek, Time, Stern, Terre Sauvage, Geo, International Wildlife, Ocean Realm* and *BBC Wildlife*. He is a consultant for documentary television projects for the National Geographic Society and the Discovery Channel, and author of *Sharks* (Voyageur Press, 1995) and *Sharks and Rays of the World* (Voyageur Press, 1999). He lives and works in Hawaii.

lenses and/or a blind. The photographer hides himself at a distance from his subject, and uses the magnifying power of a telephoto lens to make the subject appear closer. Underwater this is impossible. The turbidity of the water requires the photographer to be very close to the subject in order to avoid optical degradation of the image. This means within two meters, and preferably within one meter. Building a blind is impractical because the blind would have to be located within this two-meter range of the animal, and sharks can rarely be

predictably found within such a small area. In any case, the photographer's bubbles would betray his presence, unless using a rebreather. Bubble-free rebreathers have actually been used successfully to photograph sharks by allowing the photographer to hide on the bottom in the sharks' line of travel.

Most shark photography, however, is accomplished by the use of a method that has fallen out of favor for terrestrial wildlife photography. This is the method of attracting animals with bait. Feeding wild animals is usually a bad idea for three reasons: it can be unhealthy for the animal being fed; it can be disruptive to the ecosystem by artificially increasing concentrations of certain species at certain places; and it can be hazardous to humans—not only those doing the feeding, but also others who might come into contact with animals that have lost their fear of humans. On the other hand, it is a very effective method of attracting animals within camera range.

While it is plausible that feeding sharks is bad for them and bad for the ecosystem, this has not been proven or disproven. The topic is hotly debated based on opinion, but no studies

Armed with a Nikon F4 in protective HugyFot with Sea & Sea flash, Antonella Ferrari admires a huge female gray reef shark in the depths of Maya Thilla in the Maldives archipelago.

Below: Andrea Ferrari watches a large oceanic whitetip shark swimming over the rocks of Coco Island off the shore of Costa Rica. The favorite subjects, however, of underwater photographers in this area are the abundant hammerhead and silky sharks.

have been completed. However, there is no obvious evidence of any harm. My personal opinion is that providing food to wild animals is generally a bad idea, but in the case of sharks it has been critical to their conservation. Bait-induced shark dives provide a direct economic incentive to conserve sharks, and also allow thousands of divers to experience non-threatening encounters with sharks in their natural habitat, leading many of them to lose their fear and hatred of sharks and become proponents of shark conservation.

As for the third problem—the direct danger to humans involved in feeding wild sharks—there is certainly cause for concern. Most commercial shark dives involve a core group of sharks that have been conditioned to receive food in a certain manner. As long as the routine is not broken, there is little risk involved. But photographers who set out bait for sharks that have not been pre-conditioned run the risk of over-exciting the sharks and getting them into a competitive frenzy in which they are likely to snap at anything in their way. When doing this, it is certainly wise to take certain precautions such as having a quick route back to the boat, or to a shark cage, and having a safety diver watching your back.

Probably the most important rule in baited shark photogra-

phy is to never get downcurrent of the bait, and to never get too close to the bait supply. Once a diver becomes surrounded by the scent of the bait, he cannot blame a shark for failing to distinguish between bait and diver. Another good policy is to have all parts of the body covered in dark material: wetsuit, gloves, hood, etc. This helps avoid confusion with the bait, which is usually light in color.

Above: Doug Perrine prepares to photograph a large manta in the deep waters off the tiny island of Layang-Layang in the South China Sea. Left: Andrea Ferrari takes a close-up of a zebra shark in the same area.

A back-lit shot of a young gray shark, taken without flash. Taking good photographs of sharks and, to a lesser extent, rays requires swimming ability, enthusiasm and a measure of experience.

In order to bring out the color and detail of the shark's body, and contrast it with the dark background, it is usually necessary to use an electronic flash. The strobe unit can be a useful device to push away sharks that become inquisitive, but it also creates a problem. When it is turned on, it generates an electric field, which can be sensed by sharks through special organs in their snouts. When bait is present, sharks sometimes become very interested in such electric fields. If a shark is persistently inquisitive, it is sometimes helpful to turn off the strobe light for a while.

In addition to an underwater strobe, it is of course necessary to have an underwater camera to photograph sharks. Successful shark photography is accomplished both with special amphibious cameras, such as the Nikonos, and with regular cameras housed in waterproof cases. Since sharks sometimes swim fairly rapidly, especially if stimulated by bait, it is often helpful to use a camera with a fairly high speed of synchronization between the shutter and the flash. Some cameras will only "sync" at a shutter speed of 1/60 to 1/90 of a second, which can result in blurring or "ghosting" of the image. A sharper, crisper picture of a fast-moving subject can usually be obtained with a shutter speed of 1/125 or faster.

In very clear water, it is possible to photograph sharks with normal-view to slightly wide-angle lenses, in the 24 to 35mm range. However, because of the light-absorbing and scattering properties of sea water, most of the best pictures are taken at extremely close range with very wide-angle lenses such as the 15mm for the Nikonos camera, or the equivalent 20mm lens for a housed camera. Where it is possible to get extremely close to the shark, some photographers even use fisheye lenses in the 13mm to 16mm range.

As with all wildlife photography, successful shark photography requires getting to know the subject. Each species has different habits and a different habitat. Local knowledge is indispensable—especially the knowledge gained by divemasters who regularly dive with the sharks. In addition to being better able to predict a shark's movements and get into position for a good, close photograph, studying the subject beforehand can acquaint the photographer with important aspects of its behavior and biology, which can be illustrated in the photographs. The goal of wildlife photography, after all, is to convey to the viewer as much as possible of the nature of a wild animal.

WHEN THE GOING GETS ROUGH

The sighting of a big shark on the high seas is a situation fraught with potential danger for the underwater photographer, as proved by the recorded attacks on shipwrecked servicemen and victims of torpedoed vessels during the Second World War. An environment so hostile and so alien to what we are normally accustomed inevitably stamps us as possible prey for the mighty hunters who live there and who by the nature of things are not likely to pass up the chance of an easy meal. In the action sequence shown here—on an amateur video shot by Dr. Abdel-Rehman Al-Khathlan off the Al-Akhawein islands in the Red Sea—the author of this book, Andrea Ferrari, faces the ever more insistent inspections of a large oceanic whitetip shark (Carcharhinus longimanus). After some 30 minutes Ferrari was forced to beat a hasty retreat from the water when two other sharks of the same species arrived. The three of them were beginning to show increasingly aggressive attitudes and signs of a deliberate strategy, the prelude to a concerted attack. In such situations, the absence of any back-up protection is risky in the extreme.

HOW TO AVOID SHARKS

Being attacked by a shark is, statistically, far less likely than being stung by a bee, struck by lightning or hit by a car. Nevertheless, many sharks are by nature predatory animals, sometimes of considerable size and capable of inflicting serious injuries. It should not be forgotten, however, that we humans are the invaders of their element and that many mechanisms of shark behavior are still little known. For skin-divers in particular, here are some general precautionary tips:

1. A submerged skin-diver has less to fear than a bather. The former may look like some sort of monster, noisy and potentially dangerous; the latter takes on the guise of a pair of appetizing appendages dangling from above. And seen from a white shark's vantage point, from below, a surfer may look exactly like a sea lion.

2. Don't swim or paddle in turbid water near estuaries or outflows of organic waste or in harbors (also, and even more important, for hygienic reasons).

3. Don't go swimming in tropical waters before dawn or around dusk, the times when all predators, large and small, go into action. It is even more stupid to go for a midnight dip, beyond the protection of a barrier reef, in the open sea.

4. It has been convincingly shown that menstruating skin-divers are in no way likely to attract a crowd of hungry sharks. But avoid entering water where there may be quantities of blood from animal carcasses in the vicinity.

5. When skin-diving, if confronted by a shark that is too curious, try immediately to protect your rear; in the open sea, in the absence, say, of a rock face, position yourself back to back with your diving buddy, try to edge gradually closer to other divers, and get out of the water as soon as you can, as calmly as possible, without splashes or jerky movements. Never give way to panic; if a shark comes too close and makes a lunge, hit it firmly with your fist, aiming for the snout, the eyes or the gills.

6. If there is bait around, keep upstream of it to avoid becoming caught up in the odor given off by the food.

7. Should you encounter a shark resting inside a cave, avoid at all costs getting between the animal and the exit.

8. Always keep an eye on any sharks in the vicinity; continue swimming calmly and apply your knowledge of their behavior patterns. If they are gray sharks, pay heed to any likely intimidatory attitudes that might be the prelude to an attack in defense of territory.

HOW TO ASSIST SHARKS

Many species of sharks throughout the world are today gravely threatened by commercial fishing. It is important that we recognize once and for all that these fish are animals like any others (arguably more beautiful and more interesting) and not cruel killers. Sharks deserve to enjoy the same rights as all other creatures, and although it may not be possible to reverse the currently destructive trend, in a small way we can take steps to help the various populations recover their equilibrium. This can be done by reducing or modifying their economic importance. We can, for example, refuse to eat dishes made with sharks' fins, both in Chinese restaurants and on airlines (and official complaints, by the way, can also be surprisingly effective). The meat of the shark—sold in Europe under various pseudonyms and often passed off as swordfish—is, moreover, often saturated with heavy metals, harmful to health. Just as with products derived from turtles (soup, craft objects, etc.), travelers in tropical countries ought never to buy souvenirs made with sharks' teeth. It is also important to realize that the advertised anti-cancerous drugs extracted from shark cartilage (products of a booming industry of doubtful legality) have never been officially assessed for efficacy; and in any case, even if the validity of the active principles were demonstrated, it would be far simpler and cheaper to obtain them with synthetic chemicals. Finally, it would be of great value to support the tourist initiatives that derive economic benefit from the local presence of a population of live and active sharks; it is often former fishermen who become the most enthusiastic protectors of the animals.

Enemy or friend? Strictly speaking, neither one nor the other, for sharks are simply fish like all others. For this reason alone, they should be allowed to play their important biological role in nature without unjustifiable human interference.

1
2
3

MORE DANGEROUS THAN SHARKS

In the popular imagination, the shark—no matter what the species—is the incarnation of everything that spells danger to humans out at sea. Yet there are actually creatures far less outwardly impressive and a good deal smaller which pose much more of a threat to divers and bathers. In any event, it is always necessary to bear in mind—as we have repeatedly emphasized in our book *Coral Reefs*—that virtually no marine animals will deliberately attack a skin-diver, and that ensuing aggressive attitudes are caused most often by mistakes or carelessness on the diver's part.

Among the potentially deadly creatures that inhabit tropical seas, pride of place must go to the sea snakes, the most common of which is perhaps the banded sea krait, *Laticauda colubrina* (photographs 1, 2). This snake is a member of the family Elapidae (to which the cobras also belong), perfectly adapted to ocean life and capable of injecting with its bite a potentially lethal neurotoxic secretion. Fortunately, this reptile is more curious than hostile, with a relatively small mouth and proportionately small poison fangs; those most at risk are local fishermen who often have to disentangle these snakes from their nets.

A definite threat to skin-divers, liable to show highly aggressive behavior, is the giant grouper, *Epinephelus itajara* (3): should this fish be spotted inside a cave, it is of fundamental importance (as it is, of course, with sharks) never to get between the animal and its point of exit, for if it decides to beat a hasty retreat, the results could be catastrophic.

Much more common and likely to be even more dangerous, however, are the various scorpionfishes of the family Scorpaenidae, such as the spiny devilfish, *Inimicus didactylus* (4), the stonefish, *Synanceia verrucosa* (5) and the lionfish, *Pterois volitans* (6). All are normally sedentary creatures, often endowed with the most remarkable mimetic qualities, but their fins are eqipped with sharp, hollow spines connected to poison glands that secrete an exceptionally toxic venom. The stonefish, if disturbed, is capable of wounding and even killing the intruder. The sting of the scorpionfish will generate localized and agonizing pain, but its venom is thermolabile and its effects may, to some extent, be allayed by plunging the affected body part into water as hot as can be borne. In this context, though, the simplest solution is to avoid clambering on rocks or coral, always to take care where you are placing hands, knees and feet, and above all never to tread with bare feet on sand or shingle in shallow water. A sandy

7

8

9

bottom may also conceal the presence of a small ray with stings in the tail capable of inflicting painful wounds that are hard to heal.

Many bony fishes, too, such as the angelfish of the genus *Pomacanthus* and the squirrelfish of the genus *Sargocentron* (7), can likewise cause severe injury, whether alive or dead, if handled carelessly, because of the strong, sharp spines covering the gill opercula. The resultant wounds are very difficult to heal. However, the bony fish most feared by skin-divers, and rightly so, is the sturdy, aggressive titan triggerfish, *Balistoides viridescens* (8). Extraordinarily courageous and always ready to defend its nest against invaders of its territory, this triggerfish will not hesitate to launch a violent attack on divers venturing too close, pursuing them for some distance and profiting from any opening in their clumsy attempts at self-defense to inflict deep bites. The author has several times been its victim and has witnessed a series of concerted attacks by this quarrelsome fish; on one occasion the unfortunate diver sustained numerous bites on leg and scalp.

The banded catfish, *Plotosus lineatus* (9), a typical inhabitant of muddy and sandy beds of the Indo-Pacific, is, by contrast, absolutely unaggressive yet still potentially dangerous because of the toxic secretion of the spines on its fins. As for the moray eels (10, 11) of the genus *Gymnothorax*, they are far from deserving their evil reputation—fostered in part by the stories of slaves thrown to them as a meal by Roman emperors. They are, in fact, very tranquil and peaceable animals, but with such an impressive set of teeth they should very definitely not be disturbed, and the habit of fondling them, as some instructors tend to do at tropical tourist resorts, is at all costs to be discouraged. The bite of the moray eel is extremely painful and the lacerations caused by its curving teeth are likely to carry infection and are difficult to treat.

Another animal that should never be touched is the sea star known as the crown of thorns, *Acanthaster planci* (12), responsible in some areas for the serious damage it does to colonies of reef-building coral. The upper surface of this large echinoderm is armed with exceptionally sharp spines and covered with a toxic mucus capable of causing severe allergic reactions.

Other potentially very dangerous benthic animals are the beautiful cone shells of the genus *Conus*, which can "shoot" a poisonous dart into the flesh of a victim. Never pick one up or let it touch your bare skin! The toxic secretion injected can quickly paralyze heart circulation and may even prove fatal. Another echinoderm noted for the toxicity of its secre-

tions is the very colorful fire urchin, *Asthenosoma varium* (13), the sting of which can bring about very serious, long-lasting reactions; and the long, fragile spines of the sea urchins of the genus *Diadema* have the nasty habit of breaking off into tiny fragments that remain embedded in the flesh of the victim and may cause dangerous infection. In these instances, too, problems may easily be avoided by not making contact with the seabed, especially when swimming at night. Much more difficult to guard against—particularly for bathers who are unprotected by the lycra or neoprene body-suit worn by divers—are the medusas or jellyfish (14), especially some species from tropical seas, whose stinging nematocysts can cause very painful blisters. Less serious, though just as painful, are the blisters produced by contact with the fire coral, *Millepora dichotoma* (15), well known for its stinging properties.

As a rule, there is nothing to fear from the barracudas of the genus *Sphyraena* (16); the only recommended precaution to take against these speedy, streamlined predators is to avoid wearing strongly reflecting pieces of jewelry such as necklaces, bracelets, medallions or trinkets, which may arouse dangerous hunting instincts among the fish.

16

THE ORDERS OF SHARKS: KEY TO QUICK IDENTIFICATION

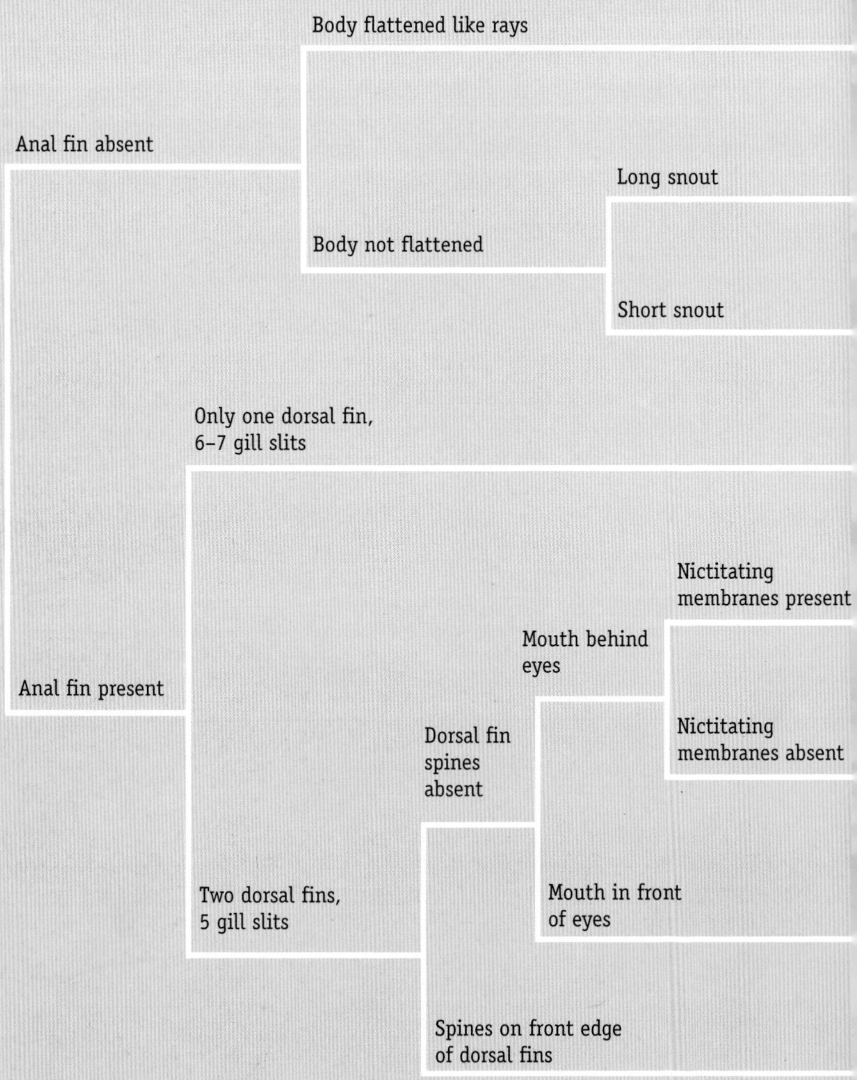

Body flattened like rays

Anal fin absent

Long snout

Body not flattened

Short snout

Only one dorsal fin,
6–7 gill slits

Nictitating
membranes present

Mouth behind
eyes

Anal fin present

Nictitating
membranes absent

Dorsal fin
spines
absent

Mouth in front
of eyes

Two dorsal fins,
5 gill slits

Spines on front edge
of dorsal fins

SQUATINIFORMES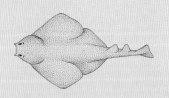

PRISTIOPHORIFORMES

SQUALIFORMES

HEXANCHIFORMES

CARCHARHINIFORMES

LAMNIFORMES

ORECTOLOBIFORMES

HETERODONTIFORMES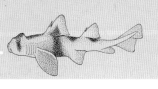

HEXANCHIFORMES, SQUALIFORMES, PRISTIOPHORIFORMES, SQUATINIFORMES, HETERODONTIFORMES

A FASCINATING MISCELLANY
The members of these orders differ greatly from one another in habits and characteristics, but because some of them include relatively primitive species (as in the Hexanchiformes), rare species (Pristiophoriformes), comparatively few species (Heterodontiformes and Squatiniformes), or theoretically more common species but typical of deep water and consequently difficult to document (many of the Squaliformes), the authors have decided to treat them together.

HEXANCHIFORMES
The representatives of this order are distinguished at first glance by the presence of a

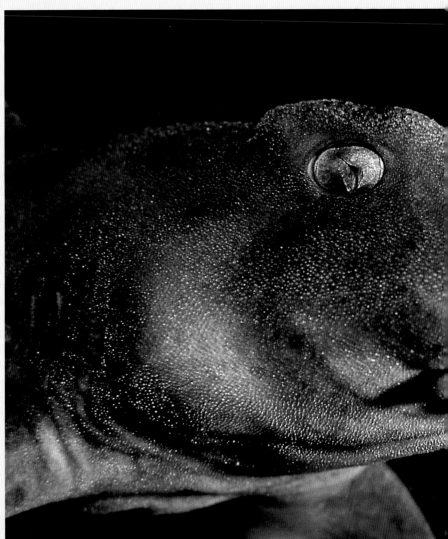

single dorsal fin, a single anal fin and, above all, six or seven gill slits rather than five. The Hexanchiformes—regarded as the least evolved of sharks—contain two families (Chlamydoselachidae and Hexanchidae) and five species.

SQUALIFORMES
Known popularly as dogfish, they are subdivided into three families comprising more than ninety species. Lacking an anal fin, they generally exhibit a spine on the front margin of the two dorsal fins. They are typical animals of deep seas, tropical, Arctic and Antarctic, worldwide. Several species are considered rare.

PRISTIOPHORIFORMES
The sawsharks comprise a single family with five species, all fairly rare and difficult to observe in nature. They are benthic sharks, without an anal fin, with a flattened body and a snout that extends into a rostrum with pointed side projections.

SQUATINIFORMES
The angelsharks all belong to one family and a disputed number of eleven to fifteen species. They are benthic animals with a very flattened body, hugely developed pectoral fins, gills in a ventral position and with the lower lobe of the tail bigger than the upper lobe.

HETERODONTIFORMES
This order consists of a single family comprising eight species. Both the dorsal fins are preceded by a large spine: the head is very big (they are known popularly as bullhead sharks), characterized by a bony crest above the eyes. The teeth are differentiated: those at the front of the mouth cavity are thin and pointed (used for seizing and gripping prey) while those at the back are broad and flat (suitable for cracking the shell of sea urchins and shells on which they feed).

Frilled shark
Chlamydoselachus anguineus (Garman, 1884)

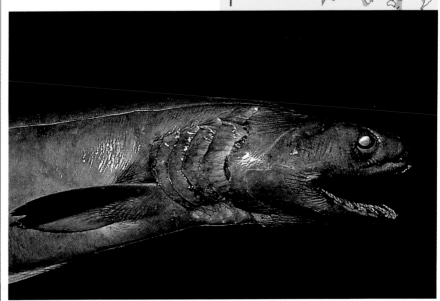

Family Chlamydoselachidae
Range Eastern Atlantic Ocean from Norway to South Africa, western Pacific Ocean from Japan to Australia, eastern Pacific Ocean from southern California to northern Chile
Habitat Deep waters, from

120 m (400 ft) to 1,300 m (4,200 ft)
Size Normally 1.5–1.7 m (5–5.5 ft), sometimes up to 2 m (6.5 ft)
Habits The only representative of the family, it is immediately recognizable by its characteristic eel-shaped body, the very long

caudal fin and a single dorsal fin. There are six gill slits (normally five in other sharks) on the short, rounded snout, the foremost of which joins beneath the throat. The gills, moreover, have narrow strips of skin similar to fringes. The color is uniformly brown. Typical, too, are the many small tricuspid teeth that indicate a diet made up of small bony fishes, cephalopods and other deep-sea sharks. It is not rare, but virtually impossible to see when submerged at the great depths at which it lives: it may sometimes be observed trapped in the nets of ocean trawlers.

Bluntnose or sixgill shark

Hexanchus griseus (Bonnaterre, 1788)

2

Habitat Very deep waters, down to 2,000 m (6,500 ft)
Size 3.5–4 m (12–13 ft), sometimes up to 4.8 m (16 ft). Weight may exceed 700 kg (1,500 lbs).
Habits It is an unmistakable species with six gill slits, small, fluorescent green eyes, and a single dorsal fin. Very strong, but sluggish, it can sometimes be observed at night near the surface. Presumably harmless.

Family Hexanchidae
Range Worldwide, both in temperate and cold waters, but seldom found in tropical and subtropical seas

Broadnose sevengill shark

Notorynchus cepedianus (Peron, 1807)

3

Family Hexanchidae
Range Temperate zones of Atlantic, Pacific and Indian Oceans
Habitat Near the bottom at a depth of 50 m (165 ft), sometimes in shallower waters
Size 2–3 m (6.5–10 ft)
Habits A heavy, highly active shark, potentially dangerous, characterized by the presence of seven gill slits and a single dorsal fin placed far back. The color of the back is gray with a sprinkling of dark spots. It feeds on benthic fishes, other sharks and large rays.

Velvet belly or lantern shark

Etmopterus spinax (Linnaeus, 1758)

Family Squalidae

Range Mediterranean and eastern Atlantic Ocean from Scandinavia to South Africa

Habitat Exclusively in deep waters, close to the bottom at depths of 180–900 m (600–3,000 ft), but reported even to 2,000 m (6,500 ft) deep

Size On average around 60 cm (23 in)

Habits The various species of *Etmopterus*—hard to tell apart at first glance—are generally characterized by a fairly sturdy body, cigar-shaped, with a brown back and typically black belly. The snout is flat, the small mouth slightly curved, and the eyes large and elliptical, characteristic of species living at a great depth. The upper teeth have more cusps. The two dorsal fins (the first much smaller than the second) bear two large spines embedded in the forward edge. There is, however, no anal fin. A number of photophores on the belly can produce a weak bioluminescence through the oxidation of pigments and enzymes, presumably for mimetic and predatory purposes. The velvet belly sharks feed on small fishes, cephalopods and crustaceans, and compete with the species *Euprotomicrus bispinatus* (see p. 95) as one of the smallest sharks in the world. Although these are typically animals of the abyss, it is sometimes possible to see them—as indeed certain chimaeras as well, likewise inhabitants of the deep—swimming around playfully, especially at very low temperatures. The specimen shown in the photograph was in fact snapped in the freezing waters of a Norwegian fiord at a depth of about 40 m (130 ft).

Pygmy shark

Euprotomicrus bispinatus (Quoy & Gaimard, 1824)

5

Family Squalidae
Range All tropical waters
Habitat Ocean depths down to 1,500 m (5,000 ft)
Size Males up to 22 cm (8.5 in), females up to 27 cm (10.5 in)
Habits Probably one of the world's two smallest shark species (see *Etmopterus spinax* entry on p. 94). Provided with luminescent photophores on the belly, it rises toward the surface after dusk to hunt the tiny crustaceans and pelagic mollusks that constitute its diet.

SQUALIFORMES

95

Greenland shark

Somniosus microcephalus (Bloch & Schneider, 1801)

6

Family Squalidae
Range Polar waters of the Atlantic
Habitat Open sea down to a depth of around 500 m (1,650 ft), from 2°–7°C (35°–45°F)
Size Up to 6.5 m (22 ft) long
Habits This is presumed to be the only shark to inhabit the polar waters of the North Atlantic. Quite rare (or perhaps, more simply, difficult to observe, given the depth at which it lives; there are no photographs of live specimens), it is nevertheless a danger to humans because of its large size and formidable teeth. It feeds probably on seals and carcasses of whales. The related little sleeper shark (*Somniosus rostratus*) is found in the Mediterranean, the eastern Atlantic and along the coasts of Japan.

Cigar or cookiecutter shark

Isistius brasiliensis (Quoy & Gaimard, 1824)

and the large eyes placed atypically at its tip. The color of the back is usually dark brown, the belly white; there is a dark frill close to the gill slits. A number of photophores on the belly can generate a pale green biolumines-cence. This species is notable for its large mouth with puffy lips and a set of very strong, well-devel-oped teeth, used for grip-ping much bigger animals such as dolphins or swordfish, and tearing off perfectly circular chunks of flesh with a violent twisting action that leaves a characteristic wound and scar. The typical bite marks have sometimes been found on transocean-ic telephone cables.

Family Squalidae
Range Very probably all tropical seas
Habitat Pelagic, exclusively at depths of 80–3,500 m (260–11,500 ft), sometimes rising at night to the surface

Size 30–50 cm (12–20 in)
Habits The body of this shark is shaped like a cigar, the small dorsal fins without spines at the front and positioned very far back; the snout is bulbous,

Spiny dogfish
Squalus acanthias (Smith & Radcliffe, 1912)

Family Squalidae
Range Atlantic Ocean from Greenland to Argentina and from Iceland to Morocco; Mediterranean, Black Sea, Pacific Ocean from Bering Sea to Chile and from Korea to South Australia
Habitat Exclusively in cold water, along the continental shelves close to the bottom, down to 900 m (3,000 ft). Found as well in brackish water, bays and estuaries.

Size 80–110 cm (32–44 in), sometimes up to 160 cm (64 in)
Habits The coloration is gray-brown back, with sparse white markings, and whitish belly; the two dorsal fins have two large, slightly venomous spines at the front, the eyes are large and the snout long and blunt. The dogfish is probably the most abundant shark in the world, even though the species is con-

sidered under threat today from commercial fishing (its flesh is widely used in fish-and-chip shops, and as a constituent of fertilizers and pet foods). Migratory and gregarious by habit, dogfish sometimes gather in shoals of thousands of individuals, but cannot tolerate temperatures above 15°C (59°F). Females have the longest gestation period of all vertebrates: up to 24 months.

Longnose sawshark
Pristiophorus cirratus (Latham, 1794)

Family Pristiophoridae
Range Temperate waters along the Australian coasts
Habitat Benthic zones of the continental shelf, in waters down to a depth of at least 300 m (1,000 ft)
Size 1.3–1.5 m (4–5 ft)
Habits The various species of sawshark of the genera *Pliotrema* and *Pristiophorus* differ from the majority of large and widely diffused sawfishes (Rajiformes) by the presence of long barbels and by the position of the gill slits, situated at the sides of the body as in all typical sharks, not on the belly, as in the rays. This species is characterized by a slender, flat body and a long toothed rostrum (the teeth being of different sizes and not uniform as in the sawfish); the ground color is beige or yellowish with darker patterns. Saw-

sharks are rather timid creatures that often remain motionless on the bottom during the daytime; at night they venture out to hunt small fishes, crustaceans and benthic invertebrates that they rummage from the substrate with the rostrum and identify by means of the long, highly sensitive barbels. Very difficult to observe and apparently quite rare, they are considered harmless to humans, but the teeth of the bladelike rostrum may cause ugly injuries if the shark is disturbed.

Pacific angelshark

Squatina californica (Ayres, 1859)

Family Squatinidae

Range Eastern Pacific Ocean from southern Alaska to the Gulf of California and from Ecuador to southern Chile

Habitat The species is closely associated with the benthic zone, at depths of 3–1,300 m (10–4,200 ft).

Size The average length is around 1.5 m (5 ft).

Habits Although it may bear a superficial resemblance to a large ray, it is in fact a shark with a large, depressed head and an exceptionally flat body with huge pectoral fins very similar to wings. There is no anal fin, the two dorsal fins are placed far back, and the lower lobe of the caudal fin is particularly large, as is often the case with benthic species. The very broad mouth is situated in a terminal position and has small, peripheral dermic lobes. The back is pale beige, with a dense sprinkling of small brown spots, forming rosettes here and there, the overall effect being strikingly mimetic. Like other members of the family, this species spends the daylight hours half-buried in the sandy bottom, hunting from ambush and bursting out with unexpected speed to engulf the fishes and squids on which it feeds. The teeth are small, but numerous and very sharp: if disturbed by a skin-diver, it will react immediately and deliver serious bites. The object of intensive commercial fishing, it is also known popularly as the monk shark and the sand devil. In the southern Mediterranean and eastern Atlantic, from Scandinavia to Morocco, it is represented by the related angelshark, *Squatina squatina*, likewise difficult to observe underwater because of its habits.

Australian angelshark
Squatina australis (Regan, 1906)

11 △ ☾

Family Squatinidae
Range Australian waters from New South Wales to Western Australia

Habitat Shallow coastal waters with a sandy or muddy bed, sometimes in *Posidonia* prairies of inter- tidal zones down to 250 m (800 ft) deep

Size Adult specimens may reach a length of 1.5 m (5 ft).

Habits Flattened body, broad at the front and taper- ing to the tail; the two dorsal fins are thus placed very far back. Active during the night, it lies in ambush by day, remaining mostly immobile and half-buried in the substrate. Capable of inflicting severe bites if dis- turbed or accidentally trod- den upon, it feeds mainly on bony fishes, cephalopods and crustaceans.

Japanese angelshark
Squatina japonica (Bleeker, 1858)

12 △ ☼

Family Squatinidae
Range Tropical Pacific Ocean from Japan to the Philippines

Habitat Sandy bottoms in shallow water, often at the foot of rocks and reefs
Size Up to 2.5 m (8 ft) long

Habits The general outline is typically that of an angelshark, very broad and flat at the front and taper- ing toward the tail. The coloration is mimetic: this is a sedentary nocturnal species, sometimes gregar- ious, which spends the day- time motionless and half- buried in the substrate. It hunts from ambush and consumes fish, cephalo- pods and crustaceans. Very similar is the clouded angelshark, *Squatina neb- ulosa*, inhabiting the deep waters of Japan and Taiwan.

Horn shark
Heterodontus francisci (Girard, 1854)

Family Heterodontidae

Range Eastern Pacific Ocean from California to Mexico

Habitat An inhabitant of the sea floor among rocks and stones, at depths of 2–150 m (7–500 ft) and more

Size Average 70–90 cm (28–36 in)

Habits This typical representative of the family Heterodontidae is a small shark with a cylindrical body and a proportionately massive head. The eyes are protuberant, placed well back, and the small mouth is characteristically folded. Both dorsal fins have a large spine on the front edge. The color is gray or fawn, with numerous small black spots scattered over the entire body and the fins. Nocturnal and solitary by habit, it often moves over the bottom by "walking" on its pectoral fins. During daylight hours, however, it is sluggish and inactive, often sheltering motionless in a rock crevice. It feeds on benthic organisms (sea urchins, bivalves and crabs). As in all the Heterodontidae, the dentition is differentiated, with small, thin but sharp teeth in a frontal position (suit- able for seizing prey without giving them a chance to break free) and molar-like teeth farther inside the mouth cavity (ideal for cracking the shell of harder organisms). Two weeks after mating has taken place, the female lays two eggs at a time, every two weeks for a duration of four months. After 7–9 months the young are born, measuring about 15 cm (6 in) long. In fact, this shark poses no threat and is quite harmless to humans; the species is often kept in captivity for aquarium display.

Crested bullhead shark

Heterodontus galeatus (Gunther, 1870)

14

Family Heterodontidae
Range Australian waters from Queensland to New South Wales

Habitat Rocky beds, among kelp forests and *Posidonia* prairies of the intertidal zone up to a depth of 93 m (300 ft)

Size Adults may reach a length of 1.5 m (5 ft).

Habits A fairly sturdy species, often kept captive in public aquariums, and notable for the conspicuous crests above the eyes, clearly visible in the accompanying photograph and the origin of its common name. It is a small nocturnal shark that rummages forcefully among the rock crevices to tease out the sea urchins, mollusks and crustaceans that make up its diet.

Japanese bullhead shark

Heterodontus japonicus (Maclay & Macleay, 1884)

15

Family Heterodontidae
Range Temperate waters of the Pacific Ocean from Japan to Taiwan

Habitat Rocky areas and kelp forests at depths of 6–37 m (20–120 ft)

Size Adults grow to a maximum length of 1.2 m (4 ft).

Habits A sturdy species, often accommodated in public aquariums where it breeds regularly, laying screw-shaped eggs that attach to the substrate with fibrous threads. A nocturnal animal, it feeds mainly on crustaceans, mollusks and bony fishes. Like other bullhead sharks, it has a bulging snout, large eye ridges, and a spine on the forward margin of both dorsal fins.

Mexican horn shark
Heterodontus mexicanus (Taylor & Castro-Aguirre, 1972)

  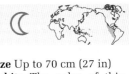

Size Up to 70 cm (27 in)

Habits The color of this small member of the Heterodontidae is uniformly brown, without any characteristic patterns; the most conspicuous feature is the large spine on the anterior margin of both dorsal fins. It is very common in the Gulf of California, where it is often caught together with other sharks. It feeds mainly on crabs and bony fishes of the seabed, which it catches by rummaging energetically among the rock crevices.

Family Heterodontidae

Range Eastern Pacific Ocean from Gulf of California (Sea of Cortes) to Peru

Habitat Sandy and rocky seabeds, kelp forests of the intertidal zone to a depth of 50 m (165 ft)

Port Jackson shark
Heterodontus portusjacksoni (Meyer, 1793)

Size Up to 1.7 m (5.5 ft) in length

Habits A typical member of the Heterodontidae, easily identified by the characteristic and unmistakable coloration of dark brown bands on a pale ground, a pattern that has made it a favorite exhibit for modern aquariums. A benthic species, oviparous and nocturnal by nature, it has a marked preference for sandy caves, where it is sometimes possible to find several individuals together. It feeds mainly on sea urchins.

Family Heterodontidae

Range South-western Pacific Ocean along the coasts of Australia

Habitat Rocky beds of the continental shelves in the intertidal zone at a depth of around 170 m (560 ft)

Galapagos bullhead shark

Heterodontus quoyi (Freminville, 1840)

18

Family Heterodontidae
Range Seabeds off the coasts of Peru and the Galapagos Islands

Habitat Coral reefs and rocks at depths of 15–30 m (50–100 ft)
Size The maximum length is around 57 cm (23 in).

Habits A small, none too active benthic shark: solitary, apparently nocturnal by habit, it has occasionally been sighted in the Galapagos on rock terracing or inside small caves on the sea floor. The species has not yet been studied in detail and relatively little is known of its behavior. Examination of stomach contents indicates, however, a diet based on small benthic crustaceans, in line with that of other members of the family.

Zebra bullhead shark

Heterodontus zebra (Gray, 1831)

19

Family Heterodontidae
Range Tropical Pacific Ocean from Japan to Australia

Habitat Seabeds with rocks and kelp forests, generally at some depth
Size Adult specimens measure up to 1.2 m (4 ft) long.

Habits Very similar in appearance and habit to the related *Heterodontus japonicus* (see page 102), but distinguished from it by a brighter body pattern of dark bands on a pale ground and by the unusual development of the two dorsal fins (particularly the first). Like all representatives of the family Heterodontidae, it is nocturnal and feeds on benthic invertebrates, especially echinoderms. If well cared for, it will adapt perfectly to life in captivity.

Cortes bullhead shark
Heterodontus sp.

20 ☾

Family Heterodontidae

Range Photographed in Gulf of California (Sea of Cortes)

Habitat Very probably sea floors of rocks and kelp

Size It is assumed that adults do not grow to more than 100 cm (39 in) long.

Habits The species is not yet classified, documented only from the accompanying photograph and presumed to be endemic to the Gulf of California. It would appear to differ in certain minor details—for example, the dorsal fins, which are markedly curved—from both *Heterodontus francisci* and *H. mexicanus*, species that are much more common and with the same geographical range. The illustrations show clearly the characteristically strong spines of enamel and dentine attached to the anterior margin of both dorsal fins of this shark. The presence of this "defensive weapon" is apparently a residual primitive feature that connects the Heterodontidae (as well as several other sharks) to their prehistoric ancestors, the Hybodontidae.

ORECTOLOBIFORMES

COMPLEX AND COLORFUL
The order of Orectolobiformes is made up of seven families (which some authors have reduced to five) and about thirty-three species. These are for the most part animals of tropical coastal waters, some of which live on the bottom. It is a complex order, containing some of the smallest sharks in the world and also the biggest of all—the whale shark, up to 14 m (46 ft) long. Among these species, too, are some of the most decorative

sharks, notable for their remarkable effects of camouflage, and hence sometimes referred to as "variegated sharks." With the exception of the carpetsharks (popularly called wobbegongs in Australia), the members of this order are wholly inoffensive animals.

MOUTH
The Orectolobiformes possess very prominent spiracles or breathing-holes and a terminally positioned mouth in front of the eyes, connected to the nostrils by a visible groove. The location of the mouth at the tip of the snout enables these animals (particularly the nurse sharks) to draw in prey such as cephalopods and fish by powerful suction from their shelters in rock fissures.

BARBELS
Another unmistakable feature of the representatives of this order is the presence of nasal barbels. These appendages of skin have a definite sensory function, for many Orectolobiformes are nocturnal. The barbels may be short (as in the blind sharks of the family Bracheluridae) or very long and jagged (as in the carpetsharks of the Orectolobidae); the latter, in conjunction with other frills set along the line of the jaws, also have a precise mimetic function, helping to conceal the outline of the animal as it lies in wait on the bottom.

PATTERNS
Some of the Orectolobiformes have colorations of delicate beauty, often reinforced by complex designs. It is reasonable to assume that these handsome patterns likewise play a crucial role in camouflage, even though certain species, as, for example, the nurse sharks, lack them completely.

Rusty carpetshark
Parascyllium ferrugineum (McCullogh, 1911)

21

prairies of macroalgae at depths of 5–55 m (17–180 ft)
Size Adult specimens may grow to a maximum length of about 80 cm (31 in).
Habits A small, innocuous, elegant carpetshark that, like all its relatives, seems to prefer surroundings of mixed algae, sand and rocks, typical of temperate seabeds. Normally it lives in rock clefts and crevices during the day, but becomes very active at night when it ventures out in search of the small benthic crustaceans that constitute its diet.

Family Parascylliidae
Range Temperate coastal waters of southern Australia, New Zealand and Tasmania
Habitat Rocky beds with

Necklace carpetshark
Parascyllium variolatum (Dumeril, 1853)

22

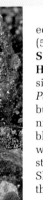

ed at depths of up to 165 m (540 ft)
Size Up to 90 cm (35 in)
Habits The species is very similar to the preceding *Parascyllium ferrugineum* but is immediately recognizable by the striking black frill, speckled with white, and the black streaks on the pectoral fins. Shy and inactive during the daytime, it lives concealed in crevices or under rocks; it is more active at night but nevertheless it has seldom been observed in its natural habitat.

Family Parascylliidae
Range Temperate Australian waters from New South Wales to Tasmania
Habitat Rocky beds and prairies of macroalgae, usually in the shallows, though it has been report-

Blind shark

Brachaelurus waddi (Bloch & Schneider, 1801)

Family Brachaeluridae
Range Western Pacific Ocean, along the coasts of Australia
Habitat Shallow beds, tidal pools and intertidal zones. Common among the madreporic formations of coral reefs. Occasionally found down to 100 m (330 ft)
Size Average length is 60–70 cm (23–27 in), rarely up to 120 cm (47 in)
Habits The silhouette is typical of a small benthic shark of the barrier reef: sinuous, with the dorsal fins positioned far back and of similar size. The mouth is tiny, with large, smooth barbels and pronounced lip folds that connect them to the mouth cavity. The spiracles are large and very conspicuous. The color of the back is a variable brown, sometimes with darker saddle-stripes, the belly yellowish, often with white spots. This small shark is difficult to distinguish from the related *B. colcloughi* and from other similar species of the families Hemiscylliidae and Parascylliidae: it can sometimes be seen in a few inches of water in tidal pools and is most active at night. It feeds on crabs, shrimps, sea anemones and small fish.

Tassled wobbegong
Eucrossorhinus dasypogon (Bleeker, 1867)

Family Orectolobidae
Range Western Pacific Ocean, in tropical and subtropical waters
Habitat Wholly confined to the sea floor, generally in shallowish water, sometimes in tidal pools and in the intertidal zone
Size 1.3 m (4.25 ft)
Habits This species is perfectly adapted to its benthic surroundings, with an overall appearance of astonishing mimetic quality. The body is broad and flattened, the two dorsal fins are positioned very far back, and the pectoral fins are large and rounded. The snout is very broad and depressed, with minuscule eyes and a big terminally positioned mouth with long, narrow, sharp teeth. The ground color is yellowish-brown, with darker marks on the back and a dense network of paler streaks and rosettes. On the front edge of the snout there are numerous dermal lobes similar to algae, which serve to render the predator virtually invisible as it lies in wait, quite motionless, on the bottom. At night it resumes activity, hunting for the wandering creatures of the reef. By nature it is lazy and sedentary, yet capable of launching sudden attacks and inflicting nasty wounds if approached too closely or—as is the case with smaller specimens—accidentally trodden upon in shallow water. For this reason it is considered a danger to skin-divers and swimmers, and there have been reports of several unprovoked attacks in Australian waters. Females give birth to live young measuring around 20 cm (8 in) in length. Taking all necessary care, it is possible to keep this shark in captivity for quite some time in suitably equipped aquariums.

Spotted wobbegong

Orectolobus maculatus (Bonnaterre, 1788)

Family Orectolobidae

Range Western Pacific Ocean from Japan to Australia

Habitat Associated with the continental shelf and the sea floor, preferably on beds of rock, coral and sandy expanses rich in algae. Sometimes found in tidal pools and in the intertidal zone

Size Usually 1.5–1.8 m (5–6 ft), sometimes up to 3.2 m (10.5 ft)

Habits A carpetshark with a broad and very flattened body, especially at the front. The snout is large and exceptionally depressed, with a number of jagged dermal lobes at the sides of the head, tiny eyes situated far back, large spiracles immediately next to them, and a huge, terminally positioned mouth with branching barbels: the two dorsal fins are well to the rear and equal in size. The coloration of the back is greenish or beige with numerous dark saddle-stripes and a wealth of lighter rosettes and complex designs. The upper jaw is set with teeth modified into long, curving fangs, characteristic of other members of this family. During the day the shark stations itself motionless on the bottom, lying in wait: it consumes fish, cephalopods and crustaceans, suddenly darting out and seizing any that stray accidentally within reach. Practically invisible in shallow water as a result of their extraordinarily cryptic coloration, these carpetsharks have been responsible for a number of unprovoked attacks when approached too suddenly or trodden on by unwary swimmers. Like the preceding species, it is considered potentially dangerous and likely to inflict serious injury. It adapts well to captivity if well cared for.

Ornate wobbegong
Orectolobus ornatus (de Vis, 1883)

26 △ ⚹ 🗺

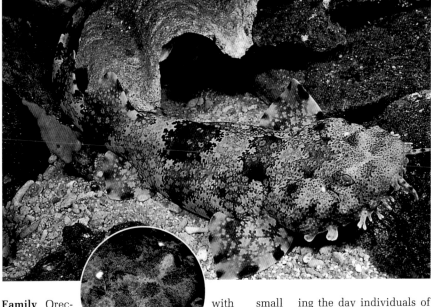

Family Orectolobidae
Range Western Pacific Ocean from Japan to Australia
Habitat Associated with the continental shelf and the sea floor, especially rocky and stony areas with an abundance of algae. Sometimes it is seen in tidal pools and in the intertidal zone.
Size Usually 2–2.5 m (6.5–8 ft), sometimes up to 3 m (10 ft)
Habits A typical family representative, the shark has a broad, very flat body, particularly in the front part. The snout is broad and greatly depressed, with small eyes located toward the rear, large spiracles immediately adjacent to them, a very big mouth, terminally placed, provided with jagged dermal lobes; the two dorsal fins are positioned far back and are of equal size. The dorsal coloration is very handsome and looks gaudy, though consisting of large black patches on a greenish or yellowish ground, and richly sprinkled with lighter-colored spots and squiggles. There are teeth modified into curving fangs both in the upper and lower jaws. During the day individuals of this species rest motionless on the rocky bottom, relying on their astonishingly cryptic coloration, which renders them practically invisible. At night they venture forth to hunt the fish, mollusks and crustaceans that make up their diet. A predator that makes use of ambush, the ornate wobbegong has been held responsible for unprovoked attacks in shallow waters, presumably having been approached too carelessly or stepped on by bathers. This species, too, is able to deal out nasty bites with its particularly sharp teeth.

Cobbler wobbegong
Sutorectus tentaculatus (Peters, 1864)

Family Orectolobidae
Range Western Pacific Ocean, particularly in tropical and subtropical Australian waters
Habitat Linked closely with the sea floor, generally at low and medium depth, sometimes in tidal pools and in the intertidal zone. Nevertheless it appears, more than other similar species, to spend more time among rocks.
Size 70–90 cm (27–35 in)
Habits Very similar substantially to the other Australian carpetsharks or wobbegongs, they are distinguishable by having a less flattened body and by the presence of large, conspicuous dermal tubercles very similar to warts. In this species, too, the head exhibits very small eyes, mouth in a frontal position and lobes of skin on the snout. The color of the back is gray or light brown, with a complicated pattern consisting of darker saddle-stripes and paler squiggly designs: the overall coloration has an obvious mimetic function and resembles in appearance a piece of coral covered with encrusting algae, contributing thereby to the camouflage effect that renders the animal almost invisible as it hunts from ambush on the sea floor. It is a fairly common species, but has not been much studied: it is known that the sharks feed on mollusks, crustaceans and small fish, and that females give birth to live young measuring about 20 cm (8 in) long. Like all wobbegongs, it has a specialized dentition for catching prey, with two rows in the upper jaw and three in the lower jaw that are bigger and longer than the others, similar to curving fangs, and which can inflict nasty bites.

Bluegray carpetshark

Brachaelurus colcloughi (Ogilby, 1908)

28

Family Brachaeluridae
Range Exclusively Australian waters along the Queensland coast

Habitat Coral beds in shallows, intertidal pools
Size Adult specimens grow to a maximum

length of around 60 cm (23 in).

Habits A timid and much rarer species than *Brachaelurus waddi* (see page 111), from which it differs at first sight by virtue of its coloration. During the day this small shark prefers to stay hidden in clefts and other natural refuges, whereas it is very active by night. The species sometimes basks isolated in tidal pools and is capable of surviving out of water for up to 18 hours.

Whitespotted bambooshark

Chiloscyllium plagiosum (Bennett, 1830)

29

Family Hemiscylliidae
Range Western Indo-Pacific from India to Philippines
Habitat Coral and sandy seabeds at moderate depths
Size Up to a maximum of 95 cm (37 in)
Habits This is a graceful, innocuous shark, much prized for aquarium display and adapting well to life in captivity when carefully handled. Nocturnal, it is difficult to observe during the day. Like all its relatives, it is an active hunter of small crustaceans, mollusks and sleeping fish.

116

Brownbanded bambooshark

Chiloscyllium punctatum (Muller & Henle, 1838)

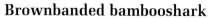

Family Hemiscylliidae

Range Tropical Indo-Pacific from Japan to Australia and from India to Indonesia

Habitat An exclusive inhabitant of coral reefs in shallow and very shallow water. It often basks in intertidal pools, where it can survive for more than 12 hours when they dry up.

Size Adults may grow to just over 100 cm (39 in).

Habits Immature individuals are immediately recognizable by their distinctive, vivid black-and-white body design; the adults, in contrast, are notable for their almost uniformly brown coloration. The shark is very timid and particularly difficult to observe in its natural habitat, often hidden during the day beneath tabular colonies of *Acropora* coral or in the crevices of madreporic formations, but it will readily bite if disturbed. At night it resumes its activities and hunts small fish and invertebrates, rummaging with its snout in the substrate. Generally solitary, bamboosharks are especially sought out for aquarium display; sturdy and tranquil, they can survive, if well tended, for up to 25 years in captivity.

Indonesian speckled carpetshark

Hemiscyllium freycineti (Quoy & Gaimard, 1824)

31

Family Hemiscylliidae
Range Indo-Pacific from Indonesia to Papua New Guinea

Habitat Coral reefs in shallow and very shallow water, intertidal pools
Size Adult specimens may

reach a maximum length of 72 cm (28 in).

Habits A species of small size, with a pattern of closely packed rust-brown hexagonal spots on a pale ground and with conspicuous, dark, rounded "epaulettes" situated right behind the pectoral fins. A typical inhabitant of madreporic coral reefs, it stays hidden by day among the coral crevices and is more active at night, "walking" on the bottom with its pectoral fins, and hunting the invertebrates and bony fishes on which it feeds.

Hooded carpetshark

Hemiscyllium strahani (Whitley, 1967)

32

Family Hemiscylliidae
Range Indo-Pacific from Indonesia to Papua New Guinea
Habitat Coral reefs in shallow water, at depths of 3–13 m (10–43 ft)
Size Adults may grow to a maximum length of 80 cm (32 in).
Habits The coloration is finely spotted, and in some individuals the whole head is darker, as if the animal were wearing a hood. Very common in Papua New Guinea. Like all its relatives it has strictly nocturnal habits.

Family Hemiscylliidae
Range South-western Pacific Ocean from New Guinea to Australia
Habitat Shallow seabeds, tidal pools and intertidal zones. Common among madreporic formations of the coral reef

Size The average length is 70–90 cm (27–35 in).

Habits A small shark with a long, slender body, the rear third of which is represented by the caudal peduncle; the snout is broad and rounded, and the dorsal fins are positioned well back and are of similar size. Immature individuals typically show black and white stripes, and the dorsal coloration of the adults is basically yellow or beige with numerous, well-separated dark spots and faintly darker bands; in line with the pectoral fins there is a very conspicuous black spot bordered in white, a clear sign of identification. Shy, with nocturnal habits and very hard to observe during the day, when it rests hidden among coral formations, this graceful and harmless little shark feeds principally on small invertebrates.

Family Stegostomatidae

Range Red Sea, Indian Ocean, western and central Pacific Ocean

Habitat Exclusively found among coral formations and especially common on the floor of barrier reefs, both in shallow water and at greater depths of more than 70 m (240 ft).

Size On average 2–3 m (7–10 ft), on rare occasions up to 3.5 m (11.5 ft)

Habits Very easy to recognize from its sturdy, cylindrical body with longitudinal ridges, the squat, rounded head with a small, terminally placed mouth, and the presence of barbels. The eyes are tiny, whereas the spiracles immediately adjacent to them are particularly large; the tail is as long as the body, ribbon-like, horizontal and actually composed only of the upper lobe. The dorsal fins are immediately adjacent and set far back on the body, the first being bigger than the second. The shark has a very handsome appearance: while imma-

ture individuals are brown with light saddle-stripes (hence the popular name of zebra shark), adults are beautifully spotted with dark rosettes at varying intervals on a beige ground (which in some areas earns the species the name of leopard shark, although this is the common name for *Triakis semifasciata*, an inhabitant of cold and temperate waters; see entry on page 156). This species is easily and closely approachable during the day as it rests motionless on the bottom, often on open stretches of sand at the foot of rock faces or on slabs of fallen debris. If alarmed or disturbed, the shark first raises itself on its pectoral fins (like an athlete awaiting the start) and then swims off with sinuous movements. At night it becomes more active and goes hunting among the coral growths for its habitual prey—sleeping fish, mollusks, echinoderms and crustaceans—which it sucks powerfully into its mouth cavity, furnished with small, sharp teeth and lateral cusps. Where humans are concerned it is sluggish and harmless, even though actively fished and probably under threat; the female, oviparous, lays eggs that are 17 cm (7 in) long, 8 cm (3 in) wide and 5 cm (2 in) thick, which she anchors to the floor with long filaments and from which the young hatch, measuring around 30 cm (12 in) in length.

Nurse shark
Ginglymostoma cirratum (Bonnaterre, 1788)

Family Ginglymostomatidae

Range Western Atlantic Ocean from Rhode Island to southern Brazil, eastern Atlantic Ocean from Cape Verde Islands to Senegal, Eastern Pacific Ocean from California to Ecuador

Habitat Commonly found in very shallow water, down to 100 cm (39 in), always in and around coral and on the bottom

Size Generally 2.3–3 m (7.5–10 ft), occasionally up to 4.2 m (14 ft)

Habits Locally very abundant, it may be distinguished from the species *Nebrius ferrugineus* (see pages 124–5)—virtually identical—by the rounded tip to its fins, whereas in *Nebrius* they are pointed. The head is broad and flat, with a small terminal mouth equipped with numerous small cuspidate teeth and externally with barbels that have a sensory function; the eyes are minuscule and there are two large spiracles. The caudal fin is very long (up to a quarter the total length of the body) and basically

formed only of the upper lobe; the other fins are large and rounded. The color of the back is uniformly yellowish-gray or beige, the belly white with rosy tints. The nurse shark spends the day resting motionless on the bottom, often sheltered by a jutting arch or in a small cave; at night it actively roams the reef in search of its customary prey (sleeping fish, cephalopods, crustaceans and echinoderms), which are vigorously sucked into its mouth. A complicated ritual of courtship and mating has been fully documented for this species; ovoviviparous, the female gives birth to as many as 28 live young. The shark is by nature shy and tranquil, but because of the great strength of its jaws, it should never be disturbed or molested. Very often, in fact, inexperienced skin-divers amuse themselves by tugging at the tail, which may jut out from the cleft where the shark is concealed. The result can be disastrous, for the animal is capable of very swift and violent reactions.

Tawny nurse shark

Nebrius ferrugineus (Lesson, 1830)

36 △ ⟡

Family Ginglymostomatidae
Range Red Sea, Indian Ocean, western Pacific Ocean
Habitat A species associated entirely with coastal waters and the continental shelf, from the surface to a depth of approximately 70 m (230 ft). Detrital seabeds, reefs with plenty of crevices and caves, atoll lagoons

Size The biggest individuals can sometimes grow to more than 3.5 m (11.5 ft), while the average length fluctuates between 2–2.5 m (6.5–8 ft).

Habits An unmistakable species (the only similar one being *Ginglymostoma cirratum*, see pages 122–3), characterized by its large size, the relatively small mouth with barbels, directly in front of the very tiny eyes, and the presence of spiracles or modified gill openings. The tail is long and partly ribbon-like, with a very elongated upper lobe; the pectoral fins are clearly falcate (sickle-shaped) and frequently used by the shark as a "crutch" when resting motionless on the bottom. The body color is uniformly gray, beige or brown, the belly white, often with rosy tints. Exclusively nocturnal by habit, this nurse shark may be freely approached during the day (though never to be disturbed) while lying motionless, sometimes in groups of several individuals, in the shelter of projecting coral arches or inside small crevices of the reef. It hunts by night, vigorously rummaging through the masses of coral and exerting powerful suction to draw in the prey identified by means of the barbels, notably sleeping fish, cephalopods, crustaceans and echinoderms. The mouth is provided with numerous small teeth, and the force exerted by the jaws is formidable, rein-

forced by the effect of the sucking action. Confined to the sea floor, from which it seldom strays, the female gives birth to live young that measure around 40 cm (16 in) long. It is normally innocuous but may nevertheless react rapidly and violently to skin-divers who foolishly attempt to pull its tail when it is asleep among the coral formations.

Whale shark
Rhincodon typus (Smith, 1828)

Family Rhincodontidae
Range All tropical and subtropical seas
Habitat Usually pelagic, it makes seasonal movements to coastal waters and specific localities, often in large concentrations. Prefers surface waters, although it is capable of diving to considerable depths.
Size Maximum length of 14 m (46 ft) but usually 10–12 m (33–40 ft). May weigh up to 15 tonnes (33,000 lbs).
Habits Diagnostic features of the largest fish in the world are the huge overall size, the enormous head and immense mouth—up to 1.5 m (5 ft) wide in adults—which opens

frontally, the proportionately small eyes, and the powerful structure of ridges down the length of the back, the lowest of which are transformed into prominent keels on either side of the gigantic lunate (crescent-shaped) tail. The belly is white, the back is gray or blue-gray, with a typical network of lighter vertical and horizontal stripes alternating with a series of white spots. Far from being conspicuous—as might appear at first sight—this coloration is particularly mimetic when seen from above, although a creature of such vast dimensions would not seem to have any natural

enemies from which it might need to defend itself. Moreover, the skin of this species is at some points more than 10 cm (4 in) thick.

The whale shark—along with other huge marine species such as the basking shark, *Cetorhinus maximus* (see page 138) and the *Manta birostris* (see page 234)—is a filterfeeder; thus, it feeds basically on plankton that it draws into its enormous mouth (which has more than 3,000 small teeth) by means of modified structures of the gill arches—horny gill rakers composed of thousands of bristles, each 10–20 cm (4–8 in)

although at certain seasons it will come into shore (India, Thailand, Australia and Mexico) where food is heavily concentrated, sometimes in groups of hundreds of individuals. This habit is exploited by various tourist organizations, which arrange cruises and trips for skin-divers keen to encounter this extraordinary creature in its natural surroundings. In various coastal regions of the Third World, it is the object of large-scale local fishing; and because the shark is slow to reproduce and even slower to reach sexual maturity (around 30 years of age), it is nowadays gravely threatened throughout its range.

long. Plankton is swallowed together with 6,000 liters (1,600 gallons) of water per hour, which is then forcibly expelled through the gills. Unlike the other aforementioned species, the whale shark is also an active predator, capable of ingesting entire shoals of sardines and even fair-sized tuna. Harmless to humans, the shark usually roams the open seas,

LAMNIFORMES

SUPERPREDATORS

This order comprises seven strongly contrasted families. Common to all the Lamniformes, however, are the presence of five gill slits, the absence of nasal-oral grooves and barbels (a feature of the Orectolobiformes), the absence of a nictitating membrane (a feature of the Carcharhiniformes), the absence of spines inserted in front of the two dorsal fins (a feature of the Squaliformes), and the forward edge of the

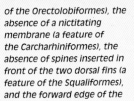

first dorsal fin situated between the pectoral and ventral fins or directly above the pectoral fins.

DIVERSITY
This group contains species that are outwardly very different from one another, such as the sand sharks or sand tigers of the family Odontaspididae (characterized by a heavy body, a conical-bulbous snout and a formidable array of projecting fangs), the thresher sharks of the family Alopiidae, (immedi- ately identifiable from the enormous upper lobe of the caudal fin), the small and rare crocodile shark of the family Pseudocar- chariidae (with large eyes and long teeth, pelagic in habit), the gigantic basking sharks (Cetorhinidae), the mysterious megamouth (Megachasmidae), the fearsome goblin sharks (Mitsukurinidae), and finally the predatory members of the family Lamnidae.

SPECIALIZATION
The Lamnidae are probably the most highly evolved of all sharks. Among its members are the salmon shark and the porbeagle (genus Lamna), the speedy mako (genus Isurus) and, above all, the legendary white shark (Carcharodon carcharias). Swift, powerful, periodically warm-blooded, these mighty sharks are notable for their massive, rigid, fusiform body, superbly streamlined and propelled by a large crescent-shaped tail.

SPEED
The large gill openings of the Lamnidae (especially of the white shark and the two Lamna species, characteristic of residents of temperate and cold seas) are indications of a broad surface of gaseous exchange, necessary for making best use of energy resources and attaining the high speeds demonstrated by these sharks.

PLANKTON
The enormous gill slits of the basking shark (Cetorhinus maximus) indicate, on the other hand, that this representative of the Lamniformes is a placid, tranquil feeder on plankton, filtered by means of the gill rakers.

Sandtiger shark

Carcharias (Eugomphodus) taurus (Rafinesque, 1810)

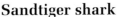

38 △ ⬠

Family Odontaspididae
Range Western Atlantic from Gulf of Maine to Argentina; eastern Atlantic from Canary Islands to Cameroon, Red Sea, Mediterranean, Indian Ocean, western Pacific Ocean

Habitat Diverse environments; usually deep water up to 190 m (625 ft), often around wrecks or near submerged peaks and rocks
Size Generally 1.5–2.8 m (5–9 ft), sometimes up to 3.2 m (10.5 ft)

Habits The four species belong to the family Odontaspididae (their classification is being continually revised) and are unmistakable, though very difficult to distinguish from one another underwater. The body is massive, with a conical, typically flattened snout and two broad dorsal fins, set very far back and similar in size; the color of the back is light brown or yellowish, the belly white, often with brown or reddish spots on back and flanks. But the clearest identification feature is the fearsome array of teeth in three rows; long, sharp and projecting

(*odontaspis* = serpent's teeth), they are even more visible because of the shark's habit of swimming slowly with mouth half-open, sometimes alone, sometimes in groups along the sandy bottom or close to isolated rocks. As it can swallow air and retain it in the stomach, the sandtiger is able to maintain neutral buoyancy, allowing it to remain motionless. It feeds on small sharks, bony fishes, crustaceans and cephalopods, often hunting them in shoals. A characteristic practice is intrauterine cannibalism; the first embryos to hatch in each of the two uteri feed on the other eggs and embryos. As a result, two young are born at a time, live, active and about 100 cm (39 in) long, after about a 9-month gestation. Basically tranquil by nature, it is generally harmless to humans if not disturbed. It is seriously threatened throughout its range despite being theoretically protected in various countries.

Odontaspis ferox (Risso, 1810)

Family Odontaspididae
Range Mediterranean, eastern Atlantic, Indo-Pacific from South Africa and Madagascar to Australia and New Zealand, eastern Pacific off Southern California
Habitat Generally in deep water, 15–420 m (50–1,400 ft), but invariably near the bottom, often around wreckage and submerged rocks
Size The biggest adults grow to 4 m (13 ft) but the average length is 3–3.5 m (10–11.5 ft).
Habits This species has an exceptionally strong body, characterized by a broad, conical, pointed nose and visibly projecting teeth. Easy to confuse with the sandtiger *Carcharias taurus* (see page 132), but distinguished from it mainly by the development of the first dorsal fin, markedly bigger than the second, and by the round (rather than vertical) black pupil of the eye. The color is gray on the back and whitish underneath; the upper lobe of the tail is notably larger than the lower lobe. Ovoviviparous, this species exhibits migratory habits that are decidedly seasonal and some propensity toward gregariousness; it feeds mainly on benthic fish and cephalopods and is seldom observed or photographed underwater because of its preference for life at considerable depth. At present, two seasonal populations have been reported, one at Malpelo (Colombia), the other along the shores of Lebanon.

Goblin shark

Mitsukurina owstoni (Jordan, 1898)

Family Mitsukurinidae

Range Western and eastern Atlantic Ocean, western Pacific Ocean from Japan to Australia

Habitat Deep waters down to 1,200 m (4,000 ft)

Size Normally 2–3 m (6.5–10 ft), sometimes up to 3.5 m (11.5 ft)

Habits This is the sole, mysterious and unmistakable representative of the family Mitsukurinidae. The snout is shaped like a blade, very long and flat, with small eyes and numerous long and sharp frontal teeth; the upper jaw is long, narrow and capable of being hugely extended outward, though normally plumb in line with the profile of the head. Both the dorsal and pectoral fins are small and rounded; the anal fin and the pelvic fins are bigger than the dorsals. The body is flaccid and compressed at the sides; the coloration of the trunk is white with rosy tints, bluish on the fins, but quickly becomes brownish in specimens removed from the water. The goblin shark is a species confined to deep waters and even today is little known. Presumably it feeds on fish, crustaceans and cephalopods, its hunt for them probably assisted by the long snout, equipped with electrosensory receptors.

Megachasma pelagios (Taylor, Compagno & Struhsaker, 1983)

Family Megachasmidae
Range Definite information lacking, but presumably all tropical seas
Habitat Deep waters beyond the continental shelf, at depths of 300–1,100 m (980–3,600 ft) during the day, and 150–500 m (500–1,650 ft) during the night
Size At least 5.2 m (17 ft) in length
Habits A huge, mysterious and absolutely unmistakable shark: the head is enormous, about half the length of the entire body, with a truncate snout, big eyes and a large, terminally positioned mouth with numerous sharp teeth, but of small size. The coloration is uniformly blackish, silvery white on the upper lip and in the mouth cavity. It is a rare species (only fourteen specimens have so far been reported throughout the world, accidentally caught by fishermen), which feeds on plankton: there seems to be evidence of daily journeys up and down at very precise intervals—frequenting surface waters at night—but it is generally confined to greater depths. It is thought that the luminescent silvery coloration near the mouth cavity may help this species—typically from the lightless world of the abyss—to attract potential prey to its immediate vicinity.

Pelagic thresher shark
Alopias pelagicus (Nakamura, 1935)

Family Alopiidae
Range Tropical Indo-Pacific
Habitat Pelagic, sometimes off atolls in the open sea, from the surface down to a depth of at least 150 m (500 ft)
Size Generally 2.5–3 m (8–10 ft), sometimes up to 3.4 m (11 ft)
Habits A typical thresher shark, unmistakable with its long tail, the upper lobe of which equals the length of the body. Similar species are *Alopias superciliosus* (identifiable when submerged by its bigger eyes), and the fox shark, *A. vulpinus* (more common and also found in the Mediter-

ranean, characterized by more pointed pectoral fins). The snout is very short and conical, with large black eyes; the first dorsal fin is midway down the back. Typically metallic gray back with white ventral surface. The thresher sharks use their spectacular tail initially to herd together the shoals of fish and cephalopods on which they feed, then to stun and kill them *en masse* with strong, sweeping lashes. This is a timid species, a vigorous, speedy swimmer, seldom observed underwater and even more rarely photographed in its natural habitat. Females of the var-

ious species give birth to 2–4 live young measuring around 100 cm (39 in) in length. Among the favorite prey of so-called sport or big-game fishermen on the high seas, pelagic thresher sharks rank as threatened species throughout their range.

Basking shark
Cetorhinus maximus (Gunnerus, 1745)

Family Cetorhinidae
Range Temperate and cold waters worldwide. From Newfoundland to Florida and from Brazil to Argentina; from Iceland to the North Sea, Mediterranean and South Africa; from Korea to New Zealand and from Alaska to Chile
Habitat Pelagic or coastal waters, close to the surface
Size 9–10 m (30–33 ft), sometimes up to 12 m (40 ft)
Habits The body is fusiform, long and cylindrical, with a very pointed snout and a large mouth. The eyes and the gill slits are exceptionally big and the first dorsal fin is large and triangular. The tail is wide and lunate, with pronounced lateral keels. The coloration is uniformly dark gray or blackish. After the whale shark, *Rhincodon typus* (see page 126), this is the biggest fish in the world. The huge animal feeds exclusively on plankton, filtered, along

with some 2,000 liters (530 gallons) of water per hour, through the baleen plates of the gill rakers. Notably migratory by habit, the sharks may assemble locally in large groups of up to 100 individuals. They probably hibernate for several months of the year in deep waters, at which time they shed their gill rakers. The liver of this species grows to a quarter of the total body weight; widely fished in the past, today it is considered under threat. Skin-divers may catch sight of it seasonally off the Isle of Man.

Shortfin mako

Isurus oxyrinchus (Rafinesque, 1809)

Family Lamnidae

Range Tropical, subtropical and temperate waters worldwide

Habitat Pelagic, sometimes in and around coral reefs and atolls in the open sea, from the surface to a depth of more than 150 m (500 ft)

Size Generally 1.8–2.5 m (6–8 ft). Bigger individuals may grow to a length of 4 m (13 ft) and weigh 570 kg (1,260 lbs)

Habits It is thought to be the fastest of all sharks—some authors say it can reach 40 kmh (25 mph)—and is capable of making spectacular leaps out of the water if hooked. Immediately identifiable, its rigid, fusiform, perfectly streamlined body tapers to a narrow caudal peduncle with lateral keels. The snout is long and pointed, with large, round black eyes. The teeth are often bared, the tail is big and lunate, the pectoral fins relatively small. The color of the back is uniformly metallic blue, with white belly. The mako shark is an exceptionally evolved predator, active and speedy, hunting mackerel, tuna, swordfish, herring, dolphins and other sharks. In larger individuals, the characteristic stiletto-type teeth assume a more triangular form in the upper jaw, indicating a diet based on bigger prey that need to be dismembered. The species—with the very similar related *Isurus paucus*—is gravely threatened by sport and commercial fishing, above all in the Pacific.

Great white shark

Carcharodon carcharias (Linnaeus, 1758)

Family Lamnidae

Range Temperate waters, sparse and localized. Relatively common along the shores of South Australia, South Africa, California and the Mediterranean. Sometimes found in tropical and subtropical waters during the winter months.

Habitat Generally in coastal waters, often near the surface

Size The maximum size is controversial, but certainly over 7 m (23 ft). On average the range is 4–5 m (13–16 ft). The weight may exceed 3 tonnes (7,000 lbs).

Habits This is a huge and absolutely unmistakable shark. The body is massive, fusiform, with very large gill slits. The snout is fairly long and very pointed. The first dorsal fin is broad and falcate (sickle-shaped), much bigger than the second. The pectoral fins are large, as is the markedly lunate (crescent-shaped) tail, with prominent keels on the thin basal peduncle. The color of the back is uniform, bluish-gray or brownish-gray, clearly distinguished, with an irregular separating line, from the white belly. Very conspicuous black spots are present on the lower tip of the pectoral fins.

The swimming action, too, is characteristic, for the body is held stiffly and is propelled by the caudal fin, the lobes of which are of almost equal size: for brief stretches the shark may work up to a speed of 25 kph (15 mph). The shark is also capable, thanks to the *rete mirabilis* (see page 40), of maintaining its body temperature at 10°–15°C (50°–60°F) higher than that of the surrounding water, enabling it to hunt much more effectively. It is an extraordinarily evolved predator (able

to detect a drop of blood in 100 liters of water), and the only shark that raises its head out of the water to look around.

The great white shark preys mainly on marine animals (frequently appearing near colonies of pinnipeds such as sea lions), but also feeds on other sharks, large bony fishes and the carcasses of large whales. It has more than 3,000 teeth—counting both the functional rows and those in reserve set along the jaw arch—perfectly triangular, up to 7.5 cm (3 in) long, serrated and extremely sharp.

Details of reproduction are still incomplete: the females give birth to 2–14

live young, each up to 1.5 m (5 ft) long and notable for their fast growth rate. Although, as its popular name of "man-eater" suggests, it is highly dangerous to humans and responsible

for a number of attacks on swimmers, the great white shark's survival is threatened, and it enjoys protection in South Africa, California and various states of Australia.

Salmon shark

Lamna ditropis (Hubbs & Follett, 1947)

46 △ ☼

Family Lamnidae

Range North Pacific Ocean from Alaska to California and from the Bering Sea to Japan

Habitat Pelagic, in very cold waters, from the surface down to a depth of more than 150 m (500 ft)

Size Adult specimens grow up to 3 m (10 ft).

Habits Superficially similar to the porbeagle, *Lamna nasus*, which is characterized, however, by a more bluish back coloration and a presence both in the Atlantic and the Mediterranean. It is a large, very active predator, often gregarious, but to this day there are no photographs of a live animal in natural surroundings; it feeds on pelagic fish such as herring, tuna and salmon. Aggressive by nature, it is often caught up in fishing nets. The Lamnidae are fast swimmers and perfectly adapted to their cold environment thanks to the development of the *rete mirabilis* (see page 40), a complex heat-exchanging circulatory system that enables them to sustain body temperature up to 10°C (50°F) higher than that of the surrounding water.

CARCHARHINIFORMES

ALL SHAPES AND SIZES

The order Carcharhiniformes comprises eight families and some 200 different species (the number is constantly under review as research continues). There is much diversity among these sharks, but among the common features are five gill slits, two dorsal fins without spines, an anal fin, and a large, curved mouth in a ventral position, more or less in line with the eyes, which have a nictitating membrane (a strong, semi-transparent eyelid that can be raised from below to protect the eye from harm). The order includes a number of relatively primitive sharks, such as the catsharks (family Scyliorhinidae), and exceptionally specialized forms such as the hammerheads (family Sphyrnidae).

CATSHARKS

Almost half of the Carcharhini-formes belong to the Scyliorhinidae, which are as a rule distinguished by their spotted or reticulated patterns and popularly known as cat-sharks because of their typi-cally yellow or greenish eyes with an elongate, vertical pupil. They are found in seas all over the world, represented by a large number of species, often of very localized distri-bution.

REQUIEM SHARKS

The most typical family of the order is that of the Car-charhinidae, composed of some 48 species. All possess a sturdy, tapered, beautifully streamlined body, with round eyes that have a nictitating membrane, as a rule without spiracles or barbels, a dorsal fin normally in front of the pelvic fins, and a flattened, pointed snout. Popularly known as requiem sharks, they are very frequently observed by underwater divers in tropical seas.

FRESH WATER SHARKS

Several members of the family Car-charhinidae exhibit a marked liking for fresh water (for exam-ple, the Ganges shark, Glyphis gangeticus, or brackish water. The bull or cub shark, Carcharhinus leucas, may swim many hundreds of miles up tropical rivers and has often been sighted in the waters of the Zambezi, Congo, Mississippi and Amazon rivers.

CONFUSION

Because many species in the Carcharhinidae are so alike in out-ward appearance, it is very difficult to identify them correctly.

UNMISTAKABLE

The hammerhead sharks of the family Sphyrnidae, represented by nine species, are all notable for the conspicuous lateral extensions of the cerebral lobes, which are responsible for the popular name and which give them an unmistakable and often disquieting appearance.

Australian spotted catshark

Asymbolus analis (Ogilby, 1885)

Family Scyliorhinidae
Range Coastal waters of Australia from New South Wales to the shores of Western Australia
Habitat Rock and coral beds at variable depths of 10–175 m (33–575 ft)

Size Adults may grow to a maximum length of about 90 cm (35 in).
Habits This catshark is handsomely spotted, with a marked capacity for camouflage. It is very rarely seen by day when it lies motionless among the corals, but is more active at night when it ventures out to hunt the small fishes and crustaceans that constitute its diet. Like all catsharks, it is quite inoffensive, even though its numerous small teeth are sharp and pointed.

Gulf catshark

Asymbolus vincenti (Zeitz, 1908)

Family Scyliorhinidae
Range Exclusively the coastal waters of south-western Australia
Habitat Beds of coral and detritus at depths of 2–200 m (7–650 ft), but normally over 130 m (420 ft)

Size Adults grow to a maximum length of 60 cm (23 in).
Habits A harmless, very shy, elegant species with a characteristically elongated body that permits it to move around with agility among the fissures of coral formations. As a rule it is hard to see during the day, and hunts actively at night. All catsharks possess a particularly slim body, so that they can literally bite their tail and squeeze into the narrowest holes and crevices.

Swell shark

Cephaloscyllium ventriosum (Garman, 1880)

Family Scyliorhinidae
Range Temperate eastern Pacific Ocean from California to Chile
Habitat Shallow sea floors, kelp forests, rock faces at depths of 10–60 m (33–200 ft)
Size Generally up to 100 cm (39 in).

Habits Typically rounded snout, typically large greenish-yellow eyes, prominent lip folds and a big mouth with numerous small, sharp teeth. The color of the back is grayish-yellow or brown, handsomely adorned with black spots. The skin is extremely rough. An expert in camouflage, it spends the daylight hours sheltering in rock cracks and crevices. The popular name of swell shark derives from its ability to inflate its stomach with water, up to three times its normal size, when disturbed or molested, remaining firmly embedded in its refuge by the additional means of the denticles that cover the skin. The females lay eggs in amber, purse-shaped cases that, depending on the water temperature, will hatch 7–10 months later to produce young about 15 cm (6 in) long. The species is harmless to humans.

Blotchy swell shark

Cephaloscyllium umbratile (Bonnaterre, 1788)

Family Scyliorhinidae
Range Pacific Ocean from Japan to South China Sea
Habitat Rocks and coral beds at depths of 20–200 m (65–650 ft)
Size Up to a maximum length of 1.2 m (4 ft)
Habits Very simlar to the related *Cephaloscyllium ventriosum* (see page 149), from which it differs in details of coloration. The swell sharks are benthic animals that feed on bony fishes, crustaceans, cephalopods and other sharks.

Coral catshark

Atelomycterus marmoratus (Bennett, 1830)

51

Family Scyliorhinidae
Range Indo-Pacific from Pakistan to China, common in Indonesia
Habitat Coral beds in shallow waters
Size Adult individuals do not grow to more than 70 cm (27 in) long.
Habits A small species, easily recognizable by its elegantly spotted coloration. Like its relatives, this catshark is active during the night when it hunts among the coral, and is difficult to spot in the daytime.

Blackmouth catshark
Galeus melastomus (Rafinesque, 1810)

Family Scyliorhinidae.
Range Mediterranean and eastern Atlantic Ocean from Norway to Senegal

Habitat Deep waters, close to the bottom, as a rule at depths of 200–1,000 m (650–3,300 ft), sometimes in shallower waters as well

Size Normally it grows to 60–80 cm (23–31 in) in length.

Habits A small bottom shark with a very slim body, characterized by an unmistakably long anal fin. The coloration of the back is usually made up of irregular black markings on a pale ground; the tip of the dorsal fins and the caudal fin is white. In spite of its liking for deep water it may sometimes be observed at modest levels in the cold waters of the Norwegian fiords.

Puffadder shyshark
Haploblepharus edwardsii (Voigt, 1832)

Family Scyliorhinidae
Range Limited to the waters of southern Africa
Habitat Generally rocky or sandy seabeds, from the intertidal zone down to a depth of 130 m (430 ft)
Size Adults may grow to a maximum length of about 60 cm (23 in).

Habits A small benthic shark that owes its common name to the strong resemblance of its coloration to that of the highly venomous puff adder, *Bitis arietans*, common in many regions of southern Africa. It is a very shy species of small dimensions, mainly sedentary, with an extremely localized distribution. It feeds principally on small fishes, crustaceans and mollusks.

Brown shyshark

Haploblepharus fuscus (Smith, 1950)

Family Scyliorhinidae
Range Restricted to the waters of southern Africa
Habitat Sandy or rocky beds of the intertidal zone down to 100 m (330 ft)
Size Maximum length of about 60 cm (23 in)
Habits Similar to the related *Haploblepharus edwardsii*, from which it differs in having a uniform brown coloration. The species of this genus are popularly known as "shy sharks" because, if removed from the water, they cover their eyes with their tail.

Striped catshark

Poroderma africanum (Gmelin, 1789)

55

Family Scyliorhinidae
Range Atlantic Ocean and southern African waters of Indian Ocean
Habitat Shallow seabeds but also rocky zones to a depth of 100 m (330 ft)
Size Adult individuals may grow to a length of 100 cm (39 in).
Habits Immediately recognizable by its typical unmistakable body pattern of long dark stripes. Exclusively nocturnal, it feeds, like all catsharks, on small fishes, crustaceans—apparently the first preference—and cephalopods.

Leopard catshark

Poroderma pantherinum (Smith, 1838)

56

Family Scyliorhinidae
Range Atlantic Ocean and southern African waters of Indian Ocean
Habitat Shallow beds with rocks and cliffs
Size Maximum length of 74 cm (29 in)
Habits It much resembles the related *Poroderma africanum* but is distinguished at first glance by the beautiful patterning of rosettes, virtually identical to that of a leopard. Shy and innocuous, it hunts at night, feeding on small bony fishes. It is often kept with success in captivity.

Small-spotted catshark

Scyliorhinus canicula (Linnaeus, 1758)

57

Size Maximum length of 100 cm (39 in)
Habits A characteristic catshark of cold and temperate waters, very similar to the larger spotted catshark, *Scyliorhinus stellaris*. The color of the back is pinkish-gray or brownish-gray with delicate black spots, also present on the fins; the teeth are small, sharp, with three cusps. It feeds on mollusks, small crustaceans and fish. It is often kept successfully for years in private and public aquariums.

Family Scyliorhinidae
Range Mediterranean and eastern Atlantic Ocean from Scandinavia to Senegal

Habitat Sandy and rocky seabeds of the continental shelf down to a depth of 400 m (1,350 ft)

Chain catshark

Scyliorhinus retifer (Garman, 1881)

58

Size Maximum length of 47 cm (19 in)
Habits Recognizable by its characteristic body pattern, similar to *Cephaloscyllium fasciatum*. The chain catshark lives on the outer continental shelf and is common in certain parts of its range while nearly absent in others (or perhaps simply fished, and therefore sighted, only where the nature of the seabed permits). Nothing is known of its feeding habits because, curiously, all specimens caught so far have had empty stomachs.

Family Scyliorhinidae
Range North-western Atlantic Ocean from southern New England to Nicaragua
Habitat Rocky and uneven seabeds at depths of 73–550 m (240–1,800 ft)

Cloudy catshark

Scyliorhinus torazame (Tanaka, 1908)

59

Family Scyliorhinidae
Range Tropical Pacific Ocean from Japan to Philippines
Habitat From depths of a few meters to 100 m (330 ft)
Size Up to 50 cm (20 in)
Habits Typical of rocky bottoms, with a handsome coloration finely spotted white. Similar to the related *S. tokubee*, found only off the Izu peninsula of Japan. It is a sedentary species and adapts well to captivity, reaching an age of twelve years in aquariums.

Tope shark
Galeorhinus galeus (Linnaeus, 1758)

60

Family Triakidae
Range Temperate waters of the Atlantic Ocean, Pacific Ocean and Mediterranean
Habitat Coastal waters, from the surface to a depth of 470 m (1,500 ft)
Size On average 1.2–1.4 m (4–4.5 ft), sometimes up to 2 m (6.5 ft)
Habits A fast-moving species, active and very timid, often assembling on large shoals and with marked migratory habits. The snout is long, the eyes are oval and flat, the second dorsal fin is much smaller than the first; the pectoral and dorsal fins are ringed with white. The back is bronze or gray-brown, the belly whitish. The mouth is curved, with triangular teeth that have a slanting edge, serrated only on one side. The tope is an opportunistic predator that feeds mainly on fish, crustaceans and cephalopods; long-lived, up to as long as 50 years of age. The species is ovoviviparous, the females giving birth to 6–52 live young, measuring 30–40 cm (12–16 in). This shark, however, is very gravely endangered throughout its range because of intensive fishing and commercial use; indeed, one of its alternative popular names is the "soupfin shark."

Gummy shark
Mustelus antarcticus (Gunther, 1870)

61

Family Triakidae
Range Australian waters of Pacific Ocean
Habitat Sandy or rocky seabeds, from the surface to a depth of up to 350 m (1,200 ft)
Size Adults may grow to a length of 1.7 m (5.5 ft).
Habit The smoothhounds (about 20 species belonging to the genus *Mustelus*) are small migratory sharks, actively hunted all over the world for the exceptional quality of their flesh. They have typical platelike teeth and feed on benthic mollusks and crustaceans. Represented locally in large numbers, all species of smoothhound are nevertheless victims of concentrated commercial fishing, which threatens their very survival throughout their range.

Leopard shark
Triakis semifasciata (Girard, 1854)

62

Family Triakidae
Range Eastern Pacific Ocean from Oregon to Baja California
Habitat Sandy or muddy beds of coastal waters, usually in shallow water but sometimes observed at depths of up to 90 m (300 ft).
Size Adult individuals may grow to a length of 1.8 m (6 ft).
Habits A timid species, gregarious and extraordinarily elegant in appearance, with a beautiful design of black patches on a pale gray ground. Inoffensive and heavily fished commercially as a result of its large seasonal numbers (with great injury to its local populations), the American leopard shark is one of the most popular exhibits in private and public aquariums.

Blacknose shark

Carcharhinus acronotus (Poey, 1860)

63 △ ⚛ ⛨

Family Carcharhinidae

Range Temperate, subtropical and tropical western Atlantic Ocean from North Carolina to southern Brazil

Habitat Coastal waters over the continental shelves, on sandy or coral floors

Size On average about 1.2 m (4 ft), sometimes up to 2 m (6.5 ft)

Habits The silhouette is typical of all the requiem sharks. The snout is long and rounded, with a characteristic dark or black spot on the underside, particularly evident in younger individuals. The color of the rest of the body is gray, brown or sometimes yellowish on the back and whitish on the belly. A relatively common species, it is considered not to be aggressive, but there have been reports of threatening behavior typical of many Carcharhinidae. Should its territory be trespassed by skin-divers, this shark will visibly arch its back, raise its snout, lower its pectoral fins and swim with an exaggerated sideways action. In the face of such behavior, it is advisable to beat a retreat. Females give birth to 3–6 live young that gather in nurseries along the coast or in the littoral mangrove swamps.

Silvertip shark

Carcharhinus albimarginatus (Ruppell, 1837)

 △ ⟨⟩⋆

Family Carcharhinidae
Range Red Sea, Indian Ocean, western and central Pacific Ocean
Habitat Generally in deep waters and around isolated banks and reefs in the open sea, seldom near the coast, at depths of 30–800 m (100–2,600 ft)

Size Females are bigger, up to 3 m (10 ft) long; males and individuals of average size up to about 2.5 m (8 ft).

Habits Quite similar to the gray reef shark, *Carcharhinus amblyrhynchos* (see page 162), this species is notably bigger, heavier and stronger, but mainly distinguished by the silver-white borders and tips on all fins, including the large caudal fin. The back is blue-gray, the belly white. A sedentary shark, it apparently has a liking for shoals and reefs at medium or great depths in the open sea over the continental shelves, where it is sometimes possible to sight resident nuclei composed of large females. Younger individuals generally prefer to bask in shallower coastal waters or in lagoons. The dentition is typically that of the requiem sharks: the teeth of the lower jaw are strongly pointed, with a serrated edge (developed for seizing and gripping prey, which consists mainly of bony fishes such as mackerel, grouper and tuna), while those of the upper jaw are extremely sharp, triangular, finely serrated and with more oblique edges (specialized for tearing off chunks of flesh after the initial bite, delivered with extraordinary force supplemented by violent, spasmodic twists and turns).

Despite the apparent lack of interest that this species shows in the presence of divers, it may sometimes exhibit curious if not downright aggressive behavior if approached without due caution.

Females give birth, after a gestation period of about a year, to 5–12 live and wholly independent young. Not much is known about the behavior or numerical consistency of the species, but it may be presumed that because it is caught fairly easily by reason of its territorial habits, this must be a cause of its becoming rare in many parts of its range. Divers can admire it in various of its tropical underwater haunts, from Burma Banks (which may be visited by boat from Phuket) to the famous Valerie's Reef in Papua New Guinea, and the deep waters of Walea in Indonesia.

Bignose shark

Carcharhinus altimus (Springer, 1950)

Family Carcharhinidae
Range Tropical and subtropical waters: Mediterranean, Red Sea, Atlantic Ocean (central Africa and the Caribbean), Indo-Pacific
Habitat Deep waters off the continental shelf, often near the bottom at depths of 240–430 m (800–1,400 ft).
Size 2.4–3 m (8–10 ft)
Habits A typical large requiem shark similar to many other gray sharks and hard to distinguish among them except by taxonomic examination (a problem common to many Carcharhinidae, difficult to tell apart when submerged). The snout is fairly long and rounded, with prominent nasal flaps. As in many related species, the teeth of the curving lower jaw are much narrower and sharper than those of the upper jaw. Typically pale gray upper body, sometimes with bronze nuances, and the belly is white, with darker tips to the fins. It is an inhabitant of the deep seas, hunting prey that includes sole, turbot, plaice, rays and other small sharks such as catsharks. Although potentially dangerous, given its size and powerful teeth, it is actually rare to encounter it underwater because of the immense depths at which it normally lives.

Galapagos shark

Carcharhinus galapagensis (Snodgrass & Heller, 1905)

Family Carcharhinidae

Range All tropical waters

Habitat Limited to oceanic islands, it prefers the clear waters of rock and coral reefs, from the surface down to a depth of 80 m (260 ft).

Size Maximum of 3–3.7 m (10–12 ft)

Habits A big requiem shark, superficially similar to the gray reef shark, *C. amblyrhynchos* (see page 162) and the dusky shark, *C. obscurus*, with a large, rounded snout, a gray or grayish-brown upper body and a white belly. There is a faint white stripe on the flanks, while the tip of the fins may be darker (never black). Common but restricted to specific habitats, along the shores of oceanic islands or in the adjacent open seas, frequently in large numbers. It often swims close to the bottom and feeds mainly on benthic fishes such as sole, turbot, triggerfish and eels, but also on flyingfish and squid. Often aggressive and potentially dangerous; if irritated it displays the typical "hunch" threat posture described for *C. amblyrhynchos*. Females give birth to 6–16 live young, measuring 60–80 cm (23–31 in); juveniles form nurseries in coastal shallows.

Gray reef shark

Carcharhinus amblyrhynchos (Bleeker, 1856)

Family Carcharhinidae

Range Red Sea, Indian Ocean, western and central Pacific Ocean

Habitat Generally found along outer limits of a reef, sometimes in lagoons

Size Females are bigger, up to 2.5 m (8 ft); males and average-sized individuals grow to about 2 m (6.5 ft).

Habits Together with the whitetip reef shark, *Triaenodon obesus* (see page 186), this is probably the most familiar member of the genus for skin-divers of the Indo-Pacific. Heavy and powerful in appearance, with a fairly long

and rounded snout, it is pearly-gray or bluish-gray on the back, and white on the belly. There is a lighter lateral stripe and a prominent black rim to the posterior margin of the caudal fin, frequent as well on the pectorals; relatively common, too, is a thin white border on the first dorsal fin, which may easily cause the shark to be confused, when submerged, with the related *C. albimarginatus* (see page 158), in which the white is much more evident. It is virtually indistinguishable, when underwater, from

another related requiem shark, *C. wheeleri* (for some authors it is the same species). The gray reef shark is a sedentary predator and markedly territorial, active during the day among the fallen debris surrounding the barrier reef, preferably at depths of 20–70 m (65–230 ft), but sometimes much deeper. It feeds mainly on reef fishes and may occasionally pose a danger for fishermen. If irritated or approached too closely, it assumes an umistakable threat posture by arching the back, lowering the pectoral fins, grinding the teeth and swimming with jerky,

exaggerated movements. This behavior is often the prelude—should the reason for irritation persist—to a brief but violent attack, not predatory but in self-defense. After a gestation of about 12 months, the females give birth to 3–6 live young, each measuring around 50 cm (20 in).

164

Family Carcharhinidae

Range Worldwide, with an apparent preference for tropical and subtropical waters. Widespread in the Atlantic, from the Gulf of Mexico to Argentina and, to the east, from the Canaries to South Africa. It also roams the Mediterranean, the western Indian Ocean and the Pacific, from southern Siberia to New Zealand in the west and from southern California to Peru in the east.

Habitat Open seas and coastal reefs, estuaries and shoals

Size The adult size fluctuates from 2–2.5 m (6.5–8 ft). The longest specimen so far recorded measured 3 m (10 ft).

Habits The copper shark or bronze whaler is quite slender with a gray or bronze back, sometimes flushed with pink, and an unvaryingly white belly. The tips of the fins are darker, sometimes blackish; a paler but not always prominent stripe runs down the flanks. The snout is fairly long and pointed, the first dorsal fin is large, falcate and pointed, with the for-

little is known about its biology. The female gives birth to 13–20 live young, each about 60 cm (23 in) long, and completely independent. It received its common name in the nineteenth century but was applied indiscriminately to sharks of the Pacific Ocean seen congregating in large numbers around the carcasses of harpooned whales hanging along the sides of the whalers. They are quite commonly seen in the seas off Australia (where a number of serious attacks on bathers have been recorded), but very little is known about its numbers and the likely risks confronting the species.

ward edge over or slightly anterior to the tips of the long pectorals. Difficult to tell apart from many other requiem sharks of the same family, the copper shark is a powerful animal, active and speedy, potentially dangerous to humans, and observable from the surface down to depths of more than 100 m (330 ft). Judging largely by the shape of the teeth, it feeds mainly on fish, small sharks and cephalopods, even though

Silky shark

Carcharhinus falciformis (Bibron, 1839)

Family Carcharhinidae

Range Worldwide, with an apparent preference for tropical and subtropical waters

Habitat Generally in open seas but occasionally in coastal waters. In the former case, it may be observed from the surface down to a depth of over 500 m (1,650 ft).

Size Normally 2–2.5 m (6.5–8 ft), although some individuals were more than 3.3 m (10.5 ft).

Habits The species is pelagic, easily identifiable by its size, the slender body shape and the long, rounded snout. The eyes are relatively large and the anterior border of the dorsal fin coincides with the posterior tip of the pectoral fins. Another key feature is the free posterior tip of the second dorsal fin, which is also much smaller than the first. The coloration is gray, brown or bronze, with characteristic metallic tones on the back due to the exceptional smoothness of the skin, and white on the belly. The top of the dorsal fin is sometimes darker, and there is a faint pale stripe on the flanks. Energetic, persistent and fast-moving, the shark is occasionally aggressive (it has exhibited threat posture when confronted by divers); it feeds on pelagic

species such as mackerel and tuna, often pursuing them into fishing nets, damaging them and for that reason is cruelly persecuted. Potentially dangerous

to humans—especially for anyone swimming in the open sea prior to twilight—it is, together with the blue shark, *Prionace glauca,* and the whitetip shark, *Car-* *charhinus longimanus,* the most commonly encountered pelagic shark. The female gives birth at sea to 2–14 live and independent young, measuring 70–85 cm (27–33 in) long; juveniles form loose groups in nurseries out at sea, entirely separated from the adults who prefer to roam farther afield. With a little luck, skin-divers can admire them at various places in the Red Sea, in the waters around the Bahamas, and off Coco Island in Costa Rica. Because it is fished so widely, the species is considered to be under threat in different parts of its range.

168

Family Carcharhinidae

Range Worldwide, in tropical and subtropical waters; in several rivers for some distance (Zambezi, Mississippi and Amazon); and in Lake Nicaragua

Habitat Coastal waters from the surface down to 30 m (100 ft), sometimes down to 150 m (500 ft). Estuaries, bays, lagoons and rivers.

Size 3–3.4 m (10–11 ft)

Habits Large and aggressive, it is responsible for many fatal attacks on humans. The body is powerful, with a short, rounded snout and small eyes. The teeth are broad, triangular and finely serrated. The first dorsal fin is large and falcate. The color is uniformly gray, paler on the belly. An opportunistic predator, it eats anything it can catch: bony fishes, rays, other sharks, turtles, birds and refuse. It is the only shark capable of surviving for long periods in fresh water, having been sighted more than 2,800 km (1,750 miles) from the mouth of the Mississippi and 4,000 km (2,500 miles) from that of the Amazon. Females give birth to 1–13 live young after a gestation period of 10 months; it lives for about 14 years; probably the most dangerous of all tropical sharks.

Sandbar shark

Carcharhinus plumbeus (Nardo, 1827)

71

169

Family Carcharhinidae

Range Western Atlantic from Massachusetts to southern Brazil; eastern Atlantic from Portugal to Zaire; Indo-Pacific from South Africa to the Galapagos and from Vietnam to New Caledonia, Red Sea and Mediterranean

Habitat In coastal waters and on the muddy or sandy bottoms of islands, in harbors, lagoons and bays with turbid water, from the surface down to a depth of almost 300 m (1,000 ft)

Size 2–2.5 m (6.5–8 ft), sometimes up to 3 m (10 ft)

Habits Easily identified because of the huge size of its first dorsal fin. The snout

is rounded, the pectoral fins are large and semi-falcate. The back is gray or gray-brown, the belly white; there is a ridge between the two dorsal fins. Spends much of its time near the bottom, which it patrols assiduously for food, consisting mainly of benthic fish and, to a lesser extent, other sharks, cephalopods

and crustaceans. It may sometimes be approached underwater and is not aggressive. Females give birth to 1–14 live young, each 56–75 cm (22–30 in) long, after a gestation period of 8–12 months. Subjected to intensive commercial fishing, the species is now reckoned to be under threat.

Blacktip shark

Carcharhinus limbatus (Valenciennes, 1839

72 △ ⍉

Family Carcharhinidae
Range All tropical and subtropical waters
Habitat Both open sea and coastal waters, often found along estuaries, in coral

lagoons, mangrove swamps and reef debris
Size Adults are normally up to 1.5 m (5 ft) although some individuals have been measured at over 2 m (6.5 ft).
Habits This species is common in tropical seas, very active and fast-swimming, often congregating in shoals near the surface. The coloration is gray, gray-brown or gray-blue on the back, white on the belly. Black tips usually present on the pectoral fins, the second dorsal and the ventral caudal lobe. There is a conspicuous white stripe on the flanks. Other characteristics that

aid identification are the long, pointed snout, the comparatively small eyes and the coincidental point of origin of the dorsal and pectoral fins. It should not be confused with the completely different *C. melanopterus* (see page 174) with which it shares a common name. Like the related *C. brevipinna*, *C. limbatus* has frequently been observed performing leaps at great speed out of the water, at the same time rotating on its own axis: such behavior is presumably associated with feeding frenzy (see page 14) when confronted by immense shoals of small

gregarious fish (sardine, herring and anchovy) on which it feeds, although it will not turn down the chance of hunting various other small sharks. Together with the related *C. perezi* (see page 176), this is the species that tourists of the Bahamas archipelago are most likely to encounter in the course of organized shark dives. After a gestation period of approximately a year, females give birth to 1–10 live young, with a length of 40–70 cm (16–27 in).

Oceanic whitetip shark

Carcharhinus longimanus (Poey, 1861)

Family Carcharhinidae

Range All tropical and subtropical waters

Habitat Almost exclusively pelagic, it lives from the surface down to a depth of 150 m (500 ft). Occasionally it may be seen in coastal waters or in the vicinity of isolated reefs in the open sea.

Size Up to a maximum length of 4 m (13 ft)

Habits The whitetip is a big shark that may immediately be recognized by its massive, tapered body, the bronze or olive coloration of the back and above all by its enormous pectoral fins with the unmistakable rounded, white-spotted tip

that is the origin of its common name. The belly is whitish, with a distinct and irregular separation from the dorsal coloring; the snout is thickset and rounded, the eyes relatively big, the first dorsal fin tall and characteristically rounded, likewise tipped with white. There is sometimes a faint, generally inconspicuous, pale band along the flanks.

Very frequently seen in tropical high seas, it is the most common pelagic shark, along with the blue shark, *Prionace glauca* (see page 183) and the silky shark, *Carcharhinus falciformis* (see page 166), and

a danger to humans: inquisitive, persistent, highly tenacious, with a majestic and deceptively relaxed swimming action, capable of sudden, violent acceleration if excited. In the presence of other species, usually silky sharks—with which it shares the same tropical pelagic habitats—it exhibits dominating behavior. Normally, however, it is solitary, congregating in large groups only when stimulated by food. Its diet consists mainly of bony fishes, pelagic cephalopods, sea birds, turtles and carcasses of marine mammals. An opportunistic hunter, it was held

responsible for many attacks on survivors of sunken ships in the Second World War. Otherwise, little is known of the behavior of the species; but for the oceanic whitetip, as for other sharks, separation of populations according to age would appear to be the rule. In the central Pacific Ocean—off the islands of Hawaii—it is not unusual to see them together with groups of grampus (killer) and pilot whales. Reproductive behavior is typically that of other requiem sharks: after a gestation period of about 12 months, the females give birth to 1–15 young, measuring 60–75 cm (23–30 in). Once extremely common, the whitetip shark is becoming increasingly rare because of being fished—deliberately or accidentally—all over the world.

Blacktip reef shark

Carcharhinus melanopterus (Quoy & Gaimard, 1824)

74 △ ⚵

x

Family Carcharhinidae

Range Red Sea, Indian Ocean, Pacific Ocean to Hawaii; also found in eastern Mediterranean by way of the Suez Canal

Habitat In very shallow water, as little as 30 cm (12 in), and in the intertidal zone, but always among coral formations. It is sometimes seen in brackish water and areas of undertow.

Size From an average length of 1.6 m (5 ft) to a maximum of 2 m (6.5 ft)

Habits Together with the whitetip reef shark, *Triaenodon obesus* (see page 186) and the gray reef shark, *Carcharhinus amblyrhynchos* (see page 162), this is the most common species of shark to frequent the coral reefs of the Red Sea and the Indo-Pacific (particularly in Polynesia), but not often observed at depth because of its habit of cruising in shallow water. Often seen patrolling the shoreline and lagoons of atolls, where it is easy to recognize the first dorsal fin cleaving the sur-

174

face, especially at dawn and before dusk. Small, slender, with a rounded snout, the tips of the fins (especially the first dorsal and the caudal) are unmistakable for their vivid black marking, all the more conspicuous against the patches of white immediately adjacent: the rest of the body is gray or more often brown on the back and white on the belly, with a visible white band on the flanks. It is shy, but liable to bite and potentially dangerous when excited: several cases have been reported of its nipping the fingers and ankles of bathers in the shallows. Viviparous, the female gives birth, after a gestation period of 16 months, to 2–4 young measuring 30–50 cm (12–20 in). It should not be confused with *C. limbatus* (see page 170) which bears the same vernacular name. Sometimes it is kept in captivity in large aquariums, but it obviously needs plenty of space to swim freely.

Caribbean reef shark
Carcharhinus perezi (Poey, 1876)

Family Carcharhinidae
Range Western Atlantic Ocean from Florida to Brazil
Habitat In the vicinity of coral beds down to a depth of 30 m (100 ft); it is apparently linked to coastal waters and the continental shelves
Size Normally 2–2.5 m (6.5–8 ft), exceptionally up to 3 m (10 ft)
Habits A typical requiem shark and the most frequently encountered within its range. The body is sturdy and powerful, yet quite handsome and splendidly streamlined; the snout is short and rounded, the large curved mouth in a ventral position. The color of the back is gray or gray-brown, with beautiful bronze tints on the flanks which merge into the white of the belly; the underside of the pectoral fins and pelvic fins, and the lower lobe of the caudal fin are blackish. The species is locally very common, often cruising along the bottom of the Caribbean reefs, and may sometimes be observed lying motionless, propped up on the sand, on rock terraces or inside caves. The shark feeds on small

sharks, rays, bony fishes and cephalopods, and is very hard to distinguish from many other species of requiem sharks, all much alike; it is similarly furnished with a shallow keel and an interdorsal ridge. Little is known, however, of its biology. Females give birth to 4–6 live young, measuring 60–70 cm (23–27 in) long. Actively fished, this is a shark commonly seen submerged, together with the related *Carcharhinus limbatus* (see page 170), in the course of organized tourist dives in the waters of the Bahamas. Normally indifferent or shy in the presence of divers, it may nevertheless on occasion display agressive attitudes if aroused by the presence of bait in the water, and should always be approached with caution.

Tiger shark
Galeocerdo cuvier (Peron & Le Sueur, 1822)

Family Carcharhinidae
Range Tropical and subtropical waters
Habitat From the surface to a depth of 140 m (460 ft), near to coasts and in the open sea. Generally in deep water by day and in shallow coastal waters at night. Often seen in lagoons and harbors with turbid water.
Size It may grow to a length of 8 m (26 ft), although the average size of adults is 4–6 m (13–20 ft).
Habits A big shark, immediately identifiable by its powerful body, the large sickle-shaped caudal fin, the first dorsal fin much larger than the second, and the broad, blunt snout. The typically handsome striped body pattern of immature specimens alters with age, turning to a uniform gray-brown on the back and whitish on the belly. Many adults nonetheless maintain visible traces of the striping that explains the common name of the species. The teeth are unmistakably heart-shaped, strong and finely serrated, nearly identical on the upper and lower jaws and perfectly formed for a substantially omnivorous diet: the tiger shark feeds prevalently on fish, turtles (the specialized teeth being ideal for splitting the shell), crustaceans, marine mammals, birds, reptiles and other sharks, including those of the same species.

The species is solitary in habit and undertakes seasonal migrations of more than 2,300 km (1,430 miles). It is potentially dangerous to humans, especially prior to dawn or dusk, and is sadly noted for a number of documented attacks on swimmers, often with fatal consequences. After a gestation of about 9 months, females give birth to 10–80 live

young, measuring 50–70 cm (20–27 in) long and quite capable of looking after themselves. The shark is more active during the night when it hunts in the shallows, around estuaries and in the lagoons of coral atolls, with an apparent preference for cloudy water; by day it usually retires to deeper waters and for this reason is seldom to be seen when submerged.

Wrongly categorized as a primitive scavenger of the seas, the tiger shark in fact demonstrates, thanks to its specialized dentition, a high level of evolution; it is able to hunt a wide variety of animals and certainly runs no risk of ever going hungry, meanwhile growing to large and truly formidable dimensions. Found locally in large numbers and often mentioned, positively, in Polynesian legend, it is often fished but does not appear at present to be endangered.

Lemon shark
Negaprion brevirostris (Poey, 1868)

Family Carcharhinidae
Range Tropical Atlantic Ocean from New Jersey to southern Brazil and from Senegal to Ivory Coast; eastern Pacific Ocean from Baja California to Ecuador
Habitat Near the surface or in shallow waters, sometimes around estuaries, bays, lagoons and ports. It descends to a depth of about 90 m (300 ft).
Size Grows to a maximum length of 3.2 m (10.5 ft) although the average size is 2–3 m (6.5–10 ft).
Habits A powerful shark with a stocky body, big eyes and a snout more broad than long. Easily identifiable when seen underwater by the typical yellowish-brown coloration of the back (the belly is white) and above all by the almost equal size of the two dorsal fins. The first dorsal originates just beyond the rear tips of the pectoral fins. At first glance it looks quite similar to the sand tiger shark, *Carcharias (Eugomphodus) taurus* (see page 132), which for its part displays a conspicuous and formidable array of needle-like teeth. The lemon shark—studied under laboratory conditions in Florida by Dr. Eugenie Clark—lives for years in captivity; in nature it is quite common in shal-

180

low waters, especially in the Caribbean. Mainly nocturnal, capable like various other species of lying propped up, motionless on

the bottom without suffocating, it feeds on fish, mollusks and crustaceans. After a gestation period of about 12 months the

females give birth, every two years, to 8–12 young measuring 60–70 cm (23–27 in). Juveniles, characterized by a very slow growth rate (the shark is sexually mature at 15 years of age), station themselves for long periods on offshore seabeds and in mangrove swamps to escape the predatory activities of bigger sharks, able to tolerate variations of salinity and even managing to migrate temporarily into fresh waters. Potentially dangerous to humans, this beautiful and interesting species fortunately does not appear at the moment to be under threat.

Sicklefin lemon shark

Negaprion acutidens (Ruppell, 1837)

Habits A species virtually identical to the related lemon shark, *Negaprion brevirostris* (see page 180), from which it differs in its geographical distribution and above all in the shape of the rear edge of the pectoral fins, which are slightly more curved. Active, inquisitive and often aggressive, this lemon shark is considered to be a danger to humans; in Polynesian waters a number of cases of unprovoked attacks, even by juveniles, have been reported.

Family Carcharhinidae
Range Tropical Indo-Pacific
Habitat Sandy or coralline shallows, from the surface down to a depth of 90 m (300 ft)
Size Maximum length of about 3 m (10 ft)

Caribbean sharpnose shark

Rhizoprionodon porosus (Poey, 1861)

Family Carcharhinidae
Range Western Atlantic Ocean from the Caribbean to Uruguay
Habitat Very shallow coastal waters but has been sighted down to a depth of 500 m (1,640 ft)
Size 80–100 cm (31–39 in), sometimes up to 110 cm (43 in)
Habits A small gregarious shark, it tolerates wide variations of water salinity and is often present in estuaries and around river mouths. It is threatened, with *R. terraenovae*, by commercial fishing.

Blue shark
Prionace glauca (Linnaeus, 1758)

80 △ ✸

Family Carcharhinidae
Range Worldwide, commonly in temperate, subtropical and, more rarely, tropical waters
Habitat Essentially pelagic, but seasonally and during reproduction around the continental shelf. Normally near the surface, but may be seen at depths of up to 150 m (500 ft).
Size From an average size of 2.5–3 m (8–10 ft) to a maximum of 3.8 m (12.5 ft)
Habits Unmistakable, the body is exceptionally slender and graceful, with long pectoral fins. The head is long, with big black eyes and a pointed snout. The first dorsal fin, fairly small, is set farther back than the rear margin of the pectorals. There are two small keels on the caudal peduncle. An immediately obvious identifying feature is the deep indigo blue coloration of the back, which merges uniformly with the pure white of the belly and which is quickly transformed into a dull, dark gray if the animal is lifted out of the water. Together with the oceanic whitetip shark, *Carcharhinus longimanus* (see page 172) and the silky shark, *C. falciformis* (see page 166), this is probably the most widely diffused pelagic shark and, indeed, with the most extensive range overall. It exhibits migratory habits: various specimens have been marked in American waters and caught in Spanish waters after following the Gulf Stream, while others have been marked in the Canaries and been recovered off the shores of Cuba. The blue shark prefers cold or temperate water and generally cruises at low speed—the males separately from the females—close to the surface. Its diet consists principally of small, pelagic bony fishes, cephalopods (particularly squid), and carcasses of whales and turtles. They often cause damage to seagoing

an evolutionary adaptation to its pelagic habitats, where prey tends to be more scarce and where it is important not to overlook any feeding opportunity. The blue shark reaches sexual maturity at the age of 5 years, and the females, after 12 months' gestation, give birth to 25–50 (and sometimes up to 130) live young. The skin of the females, subjected to the violent bites of their partners during copulation, is three times thicker than that of the males. Potentially dangerous to humans, the blue shark is today seriously threatened by the intensive commercial fishing activities to which it is subjected all over the world.

fishing nets. Curiously, it is also equipped with gill rakers, a characteristic of filter-feeders, which is uncommon among the Carcharhinidae, enabling the shark to feed as well on very small prey such as pelagic shrimps. This would seem to demonstrate

Whitetip reef shark

Triaenodon obesus (Ruppell, 1837)

Family Carcharhinidae

Range All tropical seas

Habitat Closely associated with the ecosystem of the coral reef, it generally lives in surface waters, from 8–40 m (25–130 ft), but it is possible to sight it at depths of more than 300 m (1,000 ft).

Size Together with the blacktip reef shark, *Carcharhinus melanopterus* (see page 174) and the gray reef shark, *C. amblyrhynchos* (see page 162), this is the most common and easily observable shark of coral reefs from the Red Sea and the whole Indo-Pacific. It is readily identifiable by its slim body outline, the powerful, flattened head and the blunt snout. Very evident, too, at first sight are the characteristic "cat's eyes" and the brilliant white spots at the tip of the dorsal fins and on the two lobes of the caudal fin. The swimming motion appears more obviously undulating than in other species; the first dorsal fin, moreover, is situated very far back in relation to the rear margin of the pectorals. There are two very conspicuous labial folds. The back is gray or gray-brown, often with a

visible scattering of blackish spots, and the belly is white. During the day it often rests motionless on the bottom or inside a crevice or cave, either alone or in small groups, or swims lazily along the reef. At night it is more active, preying on sleeping bony fishes, crustaceans and cephalopods, which it pursues with great vigor, often wriggling its way without injury through the gaps in the madreporic formations and even breaking off bits of coral to get at its victim.

The whitetip reef shark is often gregarious and strictly sedentary (it operates regularly within a confined area of a few square kilometers), but does not appear to be territorial; as a rule non-aggressive, it may prove dangerous if molested by an imprudent skin-diver. It reaches sexual maturity at 5 years old when 100 cm (39 in) or so in length; the species is viviparous and, although the duration of gestation is unknown, females give birth to 1–5 live young measuring about 50 cm (20 in). The shark may live for about 25 years. It is well represented throughout its range and its survival prospects do not at present appear to be threatened.

Scalloped hammerhead
Sphyrna lewini (Griffith & Smith, 1834)

Family Sphyrnidae
Range Probably all tropical seas, but also widespread in subtropical and temperate waters
Habitat It has an apparent preference for coastal waters although it is sometimes found as well in estuarine and brackish waters. It is often to be seen in enormous shoals around rocks in the ocean far from the continental shelves, from the surface down to a depth of 275 m (900 ft).
Size Generally 2.5–2.7 m (8–9 ft), sometimes up to 4.2 m (14 ft).
Habits This is the most common and most likely hammerhead shark to be encountered underwater in tropical seas. It is unmistakable, with its powerful, muscular body, the small dimensions of the pectoral fins, and the characteristic scalloped outline of the head with a broad curve running along the front edge of the "hammer" formed by the cephalic lobes. In the center of the curve is an unmistakable indentation. The color of the back is gray-brown or olive, the belly white; the lower tip of the pectoral fins, however, is black. It is either solitary or found in

immense gatherings of hundreds of individuals, presumably associated with mating rituals. Often it may be seen in remote parts of the ocean while being cleaned of external parasites close to a coral reef or interacting in a complex manner with members of the same species.

This hammerhead shark feeds on bony fishes, particularly sardine and herring, small sharks and cephalopods, which it hunts by virtue of a sophisticated, highly evolved sensory system. The form of the head, apart from offering evident advantages in gathering visual and olfactory stimuli, also has hydrodynamic functions (which justifies the underdevelopment of the pectoral fins), supporting the body while swimming and thus giving it an upward thrust. Agile and speedy, this shark is extremely timid in the presence of skin-divers and appears to be much bothered by divers' exhaust bubbles. In spite of this, it is regarded as potentially dangerous and needs to be approached with caution.

After a gestation of 9–10 months, females make for shallow coastal waters and there give birth to 15–30 young, measuring 40–55 cm (16–22 in), which stay for some time close to shore in nurseries so as to avoid being hunted by bigger sharks roaming the high seas. Although it may still be sighted in large groups, the species is deemed to be seriously threatened by extensive commercial fishing throughout the world.

Great hammerhead
Sphyrna mokarran (Ruppell, 1837)

△ ⬠⃠

Family Sphyrnidae
Range Tropical and subtropical waters worldwide
Habitat Pelagic and in coastal waters, preferably near coral reefs, from the surface down to a depth of 80 m (260 ft)
Size The average length is 4–5 m (13–16 ft); larger individuals may exceed 6 m (20 ft).
Habits This is the biggest hammerhead shark, immediately recognizable by the almost straight front edge of the head and above all by the huge first dorsal fin, very long and sickle-shaped. The color of the back is bronze or gray-brown, the belly is white.

In adult individuals there are no particular markings on the fins. Certain populations of this species (for example, off Florida and China) are known to be migratory, moving toward the poles in the summer months. Considered potentially dangerous to humans, but seldom encountered underwater, it feeds mainly on large bony fishes, other sharks and in particular on large stingrays, which it detects on the bottom by means of its sophisticated system of electroreceptors, and whose caudal spines often remain embedded in its mouth. Females, after a

gestation period of at least 7 months, give birth to 12–40 young, each 50–70 cm (20–28 in) long. The shark is often caught by big-game fishermen.

Bonnethead shark

Sphyrna tiburo (Linnaeus, 1758)

Family Sphyrnidae
Range Atlantic Ocean from the Carolinas to Brazil; Pacific Ocean from California to Ecuador
Habitat Shallow coastal waters of temperate and tropical seas, on sandy or muddy beds, often in canals and estuaries
Size 80–120 cm (31–47 in), sometimes up to 1.5 m (5 ft)
Habits Easily identified by the front edge of the cephalic lobes, narrow and unindented, shaped like a spade. The color of the back is uniformly gray-brown; the belly is white. It is fairly abundant and much studied, with marked seasonal migratory habits (it moves in large shoals toward warmer regions in winter and back to colder ones in summer). It lives as a rule in small groups of 3–15 individuals, feeding mainly on crustaceans and mollusks, which it seizes with its sharp front teeth and chews up with the flatter back teeth. Shy and inoffensive, it is difficult to approach underwater. Females give birth to 4–16 live young, measuring around 40 cm (16 in).

Smalleye hammerhead

Sphyrna tudes (Valenciennes, 1822)

Family Sphyrnidae

Range Western Atlantic Ocean from Venezuela to Uruguay

Habitat Waters of the continental shelf, from the surface to a depth of 12 m (40 ft)

Size In general 1.2–1.3 cm (4–4.25 ft)

Habits A species not much studied and not easy to distinguish at first sight from other members of the same family. Of small dimensions, it feeds mainly on small fishes and pelagic crabs. The smalleye hammerhead is rather timid and difficult to approach underwater.

Smooth hammerhead
Sphyrna zygaena (Linnaeus, 1758)

Family Sphyrnidae
Range Tropical, subtropical and temperate waters; western Atlantic Ocean from Nova Scotia to Florida and from Brazil to Argentina; eastern Atlantic Ocean from the British Isles to Senegal, Mediterranean, Indian Ocean, Pacific Ocean
Habitat Pelagic or in coastal waters down to a depth of 20 m (65 ft)
Size 2.5–3.5 m (8–12 ft), rarely up to 4 m (13 ft)
Habits The cephalic lobes are broad and flat, without a median indentation; the first dorsal fin is large and slightly falcate. The back is gray-brown or dark olive, the belly white, and

the undersides of the pectoral fins are darker. It is easy to confuse with the related *S. lewini* (see page 188), found in the same range. Very active and quite common, it sometimes forms large groups, evidence of its migratory

habits. It hunts small bony fishes such as sardine and herring, and occasionally rays and other small sharks. Females give birth to 29–37 live young, measuring about 55 cm (22 in).

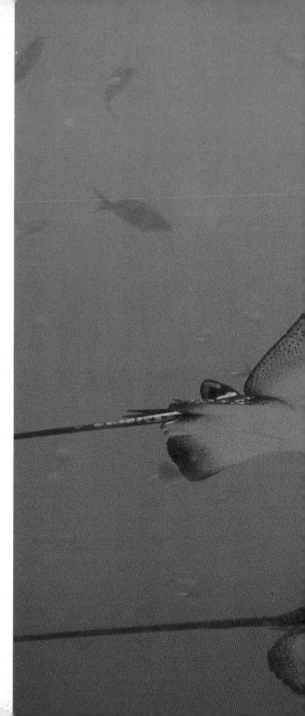

RAJIFORMES

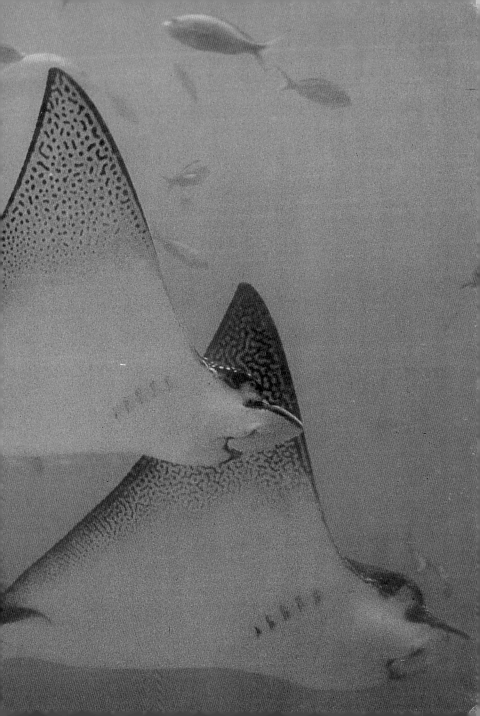

A CLOSE RELATIONSHIP

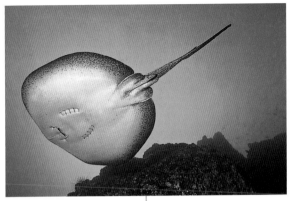

This big black-spotted stingray, Taeniura melanospilos, photographed from below, shows all the distinctive characteristics of the Rajiformes, notably the disc formed of the body and the broad pectoral fins, the long slender tail and the gill slits in a ventral position.

Some authors believe that rays are nothing more than sharks with a more or less modified body. In fact, the two forms have virtually everything in common from a cartilaginous skeleton, gill openings, the presence of a spiracle, and the structure of the fins. Other experts, however, maintain that rays are animals that evolved from sharks. The most obvious differences are the positioning of the gill slits (in sharks they are on the flanks, in rays on the abdomen) and in the characteristic flattened shape of the body, in which the broad pectoral fins are joined to the trunk, forming the so-called disc; the general resultant structure may be circular, oval, wedge-shaped or triangular. This body form—typical particularly among the members of the families Mobulidae, Miliobatidae, Dasyatidae, Rajidae and Torpedinidae—has a profound influence on the swimming techniques

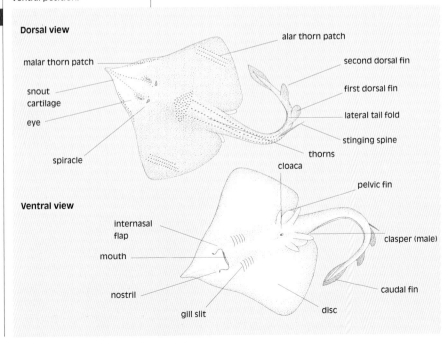

Dorsal view

alar thorn patch

malar thorn patch

snout cartilage

eye

spiracle

second dorsal fin

first dorsal fin

lateral tail fold

stinging spine

thorns

cloaca

pelvic fin

Ventral view

internasal flap

mouth

nostril

gill slit

clasper (male)

caudal fin

disc

of the species concerned: the propulsive thrust is achieved mainly by the rhythmic flapping and undulation of the "wings," rather than horizontal movements of the caudal fin, as in the case of sharks. The only rays that use the latter methods are the sawfishes of the family Pristidae and the guitarfishes of the family Rhinobatidae, which in their general body structure not by chance bear a strong resemblance to genuine sharks. The broad, flexible pectoral fins (the wings) are also used with surprising agility by certain species (especially those of the deep ocean) to immobilize prey flushed from the substrate and maneuver them into the mouth.

The Rajiformes are today divided into 18 families, with a total of almost 600 different species, often very hard to distinguish from one another; and, moreover, studies of these animals are far from being complete. Useful features for identification purposes are the pattern of the dorsal surface, the position of the eyes, the form of the snout (which is sometimes an integral part of the disc, at others wholly distinct, with pectoral fins that attach to the trunk in coincidence with the gill slits), the presence or absence of electric organs, the shape and length of the tail, and the arrangement of the pointed bony thorns that very often line the back of these animals.

A DANGEROUS WEAPON

Equipped, like the sharks, with a sophisticated system of electroreceptors as represented by the ampullae of Lorenzini (see page 24), but seldom furnished with spectacular teeth comparable to those of their near relatives, several species of rays (especially the Dasyatidae and Urolophidae) have evolved a complex defensive apparatus in the shape of barbed caudal spines which are modifications of the spines of the dorsal fin. The sharp tip and the sawlike edges make them dangerous enough, but to add to their defensive and indeed offensive efficiency, there is a toxic secretion that runs through two narrow grooves in the spines, sufficiently strong to provoke symptoms that can be very serious and in some cases fatal. In classical mythology, in fact, it was believed that it was enough to insert the sting of a ray in a tree trunk to bring about the death of the entire tree.

Associated most often with the benthic environment and the ocean depths (like the chimaeras, which are cartilaginous fishes closely related to sharks and rays but about which there is as yet insufficient knowledge), the Rajiformes, too, are in many ways still a mystery. We know for certain that—taking into account the more than 300 species that measure over half a meter—the representatives of this order are among the biggest of all living fish: thus, although extremely rare, the sawfishes of the family

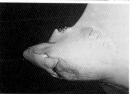

Above: other typical features of the rays are the eyes at the top of the head, the large spiracle immediately adjacent, the ventrally situated mouth and, in many species, the presence of venomous spines at the base of the tail. Facing page: the external anatomy of rays.

The extraordinary elegant and powerful swimming action of the manta, Manta birostris, *is created largely by the broad pectoral fins that are used for propulsion virtually like wings and the ventrally positioned gill slits.*

Pristidae may measure more than 7 m (23 ft) in length, while up to a few decades ago it was not uncommon to come across mantas of *Manta birostris* with a "wingspan" of 7 m (23 ft) and a weight of several tonnes. Moreover, of all the cartilaginous fishes it is the rays that can boast the highest "intelligence;" the ratio between the mass of the brain and of the body is comparable to that found in birds, reaching its optimum in the manta itself (as is recognized by any skin-divers who have happened to experience personally the touching curiosity that impels this huge fish to approach them closely underwater and sometimes even to keep them company for some length of time).

Distributed in seas and oceans throughout the world (and represented by many species of the genus *Potamotrygon* even in the tropical fresh waters of South America), rays would appear to be descended in direct line from the sharks: the sawfishes and guitarfishes may constitute the most archaic of these families, whereas devil rays and stingrays could be of more recent evolution. Predators perfectly adapted to their surroundings— be it pelagic desert or soft sandy bottom—and able to move around underwater even more elegantly than sharks, many rays are today, like their closest relatives, gravely imperiled by wide-scale and completely unregulated commercial fishing.

CHIMAERAS

Known also as ghost sharks or ratfishes, the chimaeras are cartilaginous fishes that appeared 400 million years ago, during the Devonian period, but stem from a different evolutionary line. Lacking a swim bladder and having a cartilaginous skeleton like sharks and rays, chimaeras differ by having the jaw attached to the cranium (holostylic), gill slits covered by a single fold of skin (thus with a single external opening), no spiracle and typically smooth, "naked" skin (without dermal denticles). The first dorsal fin is mobile, with a long spine often connected to a venom gland; the body is fusiform, narrowing at the rear to a threadlike tail. The dentition consists of numerous grinding plates, indicating a diet of small deep-sea fishes, mollusks and cephalopods.

Chimaeras are characteristic creatures of the depths and are divided into three families: Chimaeridae or shortnose chimaeras (two genera, *Hydrolagus* and *Chimaera*, and about 21 species); Callorhinchidae or elephant chimaeras (one genus, *Callorhynchus*, and four species); and Rhinochimaeridae or longnose chimaeras (three genera, *Rhinochimaera*, *Harriotta* and *Neoharriotta*, totaling six species).

199

Like many other large-sized pelagic species, manta rays are animals that feed by filtering plankton. Under favorable conditions, when there is plenty of food available, it is not unusual to observe up to fifteen of them together.

THE FAMILIES OF RAYS: KEY TO QUICK IDENTIFICATION

Sawlike snout

Two dorsal fins, the first nearer to the pelvic fins than to the tail tip

Electric organs absent

Electric organs present

Not sawlike snout

Two dorsal fins, the first nearer to the tail tip than to the pelvic fins

Pelvic fin divided into two lobes

Head incorporated in the disc

Pelvic fin with one lobe

Head partially separate

PRISTIDAE

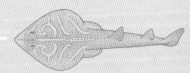

RHINOBATIDAE

TORPEDINIDAE

201

RAJIDAE

DASYATIDAE

MYLIOBATIDAE AND
MOBULIDAE

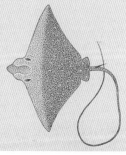

Smalltooth sawfish

Pristis pectinata (Latham, 1794)

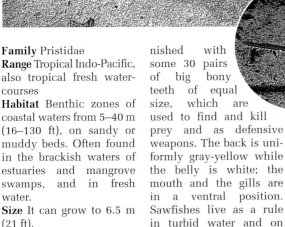

Family Pristidae

Range Tropical Indo-Pacific, also tropical fresh water-courses

Habitat Benthic zones of coastal waters from 5–40 m (16–130 ft), on sandy or muddy beds. Often found in the brackish waters of estuaries and mangrove swamps, and in fresh water.

Size It can grow to 6.5 m (21 ft).

Habits In contrast to other rays, the sawfishes are characterized by an elongate body and fins (both dorsals and caudal) similar to those of true sharks. A diagnostic feature is the long frontal rostrum, furnished with some 30 pairs of big bony teeth of equal size, which are used to find and kill prey and as defensive weapons. The back is uniformly gray-yellow while the belly is white; the mouth and the gills are in a ventral position. Sawfishes live as a rule in turbid water and on sandy and muddy bottoms, preferring brackish waters. Gravely threatened with extinction throughout their range, they are among the biggest fish in the world. Given their life-styles and frequented habitats, they are virtually impossible animals to encounter in the course of normal sporting dives, and in any case, the poor visibility in tropical rivers and estuaries makes it equally impossible to photograph them (the pictures accompanying this entry are in fact of an immature specimen in a public aquarium). It may happen, though, that individuals are from time to time caught up in fishermen's nets, especially in the major rivers of Borneo.

Bowmouth guitarfish or shark ray
Rhina ancylostoma (Bloch & Schneider, 1801)

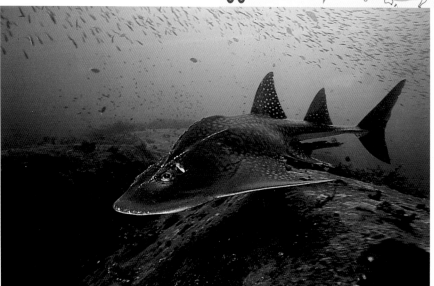

Family Rhinobatidae
Range Tropical Indo-Pacific
Habitat Sandy beds in coastal waters and on coral reefs in the open sea, up to a depth of 90 m (300 ft).
Size Up to 3 m (10 ft) long
Habits A guitarfish of unmistakable shape, similar to a true shark both in general outline and style of swimming. The body is very powerful, with the back strikingly arched and traversed by long horny keels, equipped with sharp spiky thorns; the fins, including the caudal, are large and pointed, the mouth typically curved and situated underneath, as are the gill slits. The coloration of the back is dark gray, finely dotted with lighter spots that become more dense toward the tail. The appearance of this large fish is truly impressive; it is sedentary but not territorial, and is most active at night. It feeds principally on fish, mollusks and crustaceans. It is much sought after locally by fishermen and is considered to be seriously under threat.

Family Rhinobatidae

Range Tropical Indo-Pacific

Habitat Usually on sandy bottoms in coastal waters and on barrier reefs in the open sea, down to a depth of 50 m (165 ft)

Size Up to a length of 3 m (10 ft) and a weight of over 220 kg (480 lbs)

Habits A massive, elongated ray, its rear part very like that of a shark and with a similar swimming action. The two dorsal fins are tall, pointed and falcate, the tail is lunate; the snout is long, pointed and very flat, with the mouth in a ventral position. The coloration of the back is very variable, generally yellowish, beige or black, often with a scattering of small white spots and two black ocelli on the pectorals. Locally common, the ray is as a rule timid but sometimes fascinated by divers, approaching them rapidly for a fleeting examination. In the Atlantic and the Caribbean the genus is represented by several species more or less alike, but of smaller dimensions. The Rhinobatidae feed on fish and benthic organisms; females give birth to 6–30 live young.

Eastern fiddler ray

Trygonorrhina fasciata (Muller & Henle, 1841)

Family Rhinobatidae

Range Exclusively along the Australian coasts of southern Queensland to Victoria

Habitat Sandy seabeds and areas of seagrass and *Posidonia*, and often, too, near rocky coral reefs, down to a depth of 180 m (600 ft).

Size Adults may grow to a maximum length of 1.3 m (4.25 ft).

Habits A characteristic ray of Australian coastal waters, recognizable by the broad, rounded pectoral fins and the typical network of pale stripes on the back. Very similar are the southern fiddler ray, *T. fasciata guanerius*, whose dorsal ornamentation is slightly different, and two others, not yet classified (and probably chromatic variations of the same species), one with the pectoral fins bordered white and the other entirely bluish-black and known locally as the magpie fiddler ray. Although these rays are fairly common locally and of quite conspicuous appearance, the rays of the genus *Trygonorrhina* have so far been little studied: almost nothing is known about the present numbers of the various species, nor of their feeding habits and the likely risks they face from human interference. All the members of this genus are readily distinguished at first glance from those of the genus *Aptychotrema* (with which they share a geographical range: see page 206) by the snout, which is more rounded and less obviously separated from the body.

Western shovelnose ray

Aptychotrema vincentiana (Haacke, 1885)

91

and *Posidonia* prairies
Size It may grow to a maximum length of about 100 cm (39 in).

Habits Very similar to the related *Aptychotrema bougainvillii*, from which it differs by reason of a shorter snout and more conspicuous markings on the back. The female gives birth to up to eight live young.

Family Rhinobatidae
Range Confined to Australian waters, from Queens-
land to New South Wales
Habitat Sandy seabeds near cliffs, shallow bays

Eastern shovelnose ray

Aptychotrema rostrata (Shaw & Nodder, 1794)

92

than 60 m (200 ft)
Size The biggest individuals grow to a length of 1.2 m (4 ft).

Habits A species that has not been widely studied but which is apparently common on the beds of shallow bays and estuaries, often close to rocks. The female gives birth to up to four live young.

Family Rhinobatidae
Range Exclusively Australian waters, from Queensland to Victoria
Habitat On sandy bottoms and in *Posidonia* prairies, from the intertidal zone down to a depth of more

Pacific electric ray
Torpedo californica (Ayres, 1855)

93 △ ☾

Family Torpedinidae
Range Temperate waters of the Pacific Ocean from British Columbia to Baja California
Habitat Sandy bottoms at depths of 3–196 m (10–650 ft)
Size Maximum length of 1.4 m (4.5 ft)
Habits This large electric ray has nocturnal habits and spends the daytime submerged in the sandy substrate. Solitary and locally common, it is nomadic though not migratory; it catches its prey (small fish) by stunning them with a strong electric shock. It looks quite inconspicuous in its habitat and will float motionless in a column of water. Shy, but surprisingly aggressive if provoked, it is prompt to react and attack an intruder, and is therefore potentially dangerous. The color of the back is gray with a scattering of black spots: a very similar species is the Japanese electric ray, *T. tokionis*, entirely black or brownish, and so far only sighted in Japanese waters.

208

Family Hypnidae

Range Exclusively in Australian temperate and subtropical waters

Habitat A benthic species of coastal waters down to a depth of 220 m (720 ft), on sandy and muddy floors. Often found, too, in estuaries and mangrove swamps.

Size A non-aggressive but dangerous electric ray, capable of delivering electric shocks with suitably developed organs situated in the center of the pectoral fins. The body is typically flattened, with very small eyes and spiracles in a dorsal position: when seen from above its silhouette is something like that of a coffin, particularly in the case of specimens beached following a storm, and hence its common name. The tail is extraordinarily short, surmounted by two tiny dorsal fins. The coloration of the back is strikingly mimetic, with thin markings against a light brown, pale gray or pinkish ground, astonishingly similar to the surface of the sand in which the ray buries itself completely during the day. It will even change color to heighten the effect of camouflage, and for that reason is almost impossible to see. Viviparous, it feeds on fish and benthic organisms.

Cortes electric ray

Narcine entemedor (Jordan & Starks, 1895)

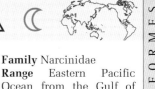

Family Narcinidae
Range Eastern Pacific Ocean from the Gulf of California to Panama
Habitat Sandy beds in shallow waters
Size Grows to a length of 76 cm (30 in) long
Habits Nocturnal, normally half-buried in the substrate during the day. If disturbed it exhibits a characteristic strategy against predators, "exploding" from the bottom, arching its back and then doing a "somersault" in a column of water. It feeds mainly on polychaete worms.

Lesser electric ray

Narcine brasiliensis (Olfers, 1831)

Size Grows to just over 45 cm (18 in) long
Habits Nocturnal, this species is much studied for biology courses in U.S. universities. By day it remains motionless, usually half-buried in the substrate; at night, when hunting, it is much more active. Fairly common along the coastal belt, its diet consists almost wholly of worms and small crustaceans. In winter it migrates to greater depths, forming groups. As in many cartilaginous fishes, the juvenile has brighter colors than the adults.

Family Narcinidae
Range Atlantic Ocean from North Carolina to the coasts of Argentina

Habitat Sandy beds in shallow waters, from the surface down to a depth of 40 m (130 ft)

Bulls-eye electric ray

Diplobatus ommata (Jordan & Gilbert, 1890)

△ ☾

Size Adult specimens grow to a length of no more than 25 cm (10 in).

Habits This species, sluggish and inactive by day, moves at night by "hopping" along the bottom on its pectoral fins, hunting the worms and shrimps that make up its diet. The very similar *Diplobatus pictus* is found along the South American shores of the Atlantic Ocean. Some authors classify the latter species as *D. picta*.

Family Narcinidae
Range Eastern Pacific Ocean from the Gulf of California to Panama

Habitat Sea floors of sand or detritus from the intertidal zone to a depth of 65 m (210 ft)

Smooth stingray

Dasyatis brevicaudata (Hutton, 1875)

depth of more than 470 m (1,540 ft)

Size Adult specimens grow to a width of over 2 m (6.5 ft).

Habits A relatively common stingray of coastal waters, sandy and muddy beds of estuaries, bays and harbors, and near rocky reefs. It feeds on fish, bivalves, mollusks and crustaceans. This big species often forms large groups made up of dozens of individuals that make for the coastal shallows with the arrival of high tide.

Family Dasyatidae
Range Indian Ocean along the African coasts; also present in Australian and

New Zealand waters
Habitat Bottoms of sand, mud and detritus from the intertidal zone down to a

Roughtail stingray
Dasyatis centroura (Mitchell, 1815)

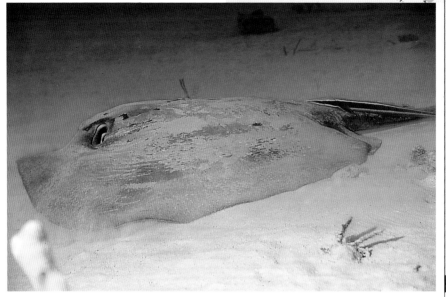

Family Dasyatidae

Range Temperate and sub-tropical Atlantic Ocean, Mediterranean

Habitat Sandy and muddy beds in coastal waters, down to a depth of more than 60 m (200 ft)

Size Up to a length of 2.2 m (7 ft)

Habits A gigantic stingray difficult to see when submerged and at first glance identical to the southern stingray, *Dasyatis americana* (see page 218), from which it may be distinguished by the numerous spiny tubercles on the back and along the tail. The body is very thick and heavy, with small eyes set high and prominent spiracles; the tail is muscular, especially near the juncture with the disc, and has one or two large serrated, venomous spines. The back is generally gray, brown or black, the belly white. Shy, but sometimes approach-able underwater when resting motionless on the bottom, half-buried in the sand. Another similar stingray is *Dasyatis schmardae*, lacking spiny tubercles and restricted to a range in the southern Caribbean.

Black-spotted stingray
Taeniura melanospilos (Muller & Henle, 1841)

100 △ ⟨⟩

Family Dasyatidae
Range Tropical latitudes of Indian Ocean and Pacific Ocean
Habitat Relatively common in waters at medium depths of 20 m (65 ft) and more, on

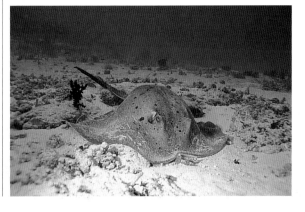

sandy beds in the vicinity of rock terraces and debris; also often in caves or beneath jutting rocks
Size As a rule 1.5–2 m (5–6.5 ft) but may grow to 3 m (10 ft), including tail.

Habits The black-spotted stingray is a large and highly spectacular species, easily identifiable when submerged by the striking thickness of its body and the discoid structure typical of all representatives of this family. The coloration of the back is highly variable, usually light to dark gray, sometimes almost black, but always finely speckled or streaked with black; the belly is white, often dotted with darker marks. The eyes are small, set high; there is a large spiracle immediately behind the eye cavity. Solitary or in small groups, the ray usually remains motion-

with serrated edges set close to the base of the tail: if molested it arches the back and lifts the tail, exposing the forward-facing spine and giving it a characteristic wave to and fro, which is often the prelude to a whiplike stinging action, very painful and sometimes with fatal consequences. If undisturbed, however, it is absolutely innocuous and unaggressive. Together with the smaller and more colorful blue-spotted ribbontail ray, *Taeniura lymma* (see page 214), it is very frequently sighted by skin-divers in Indo-Pacific waters.

less in the sand at the base of reef walls during the day, and hunts small fishes, crustaceans, mollusks and benthic organisms, blowing powerfully at the sandy substrate to extract them. This species is equipped with one or two strong, venomous spines

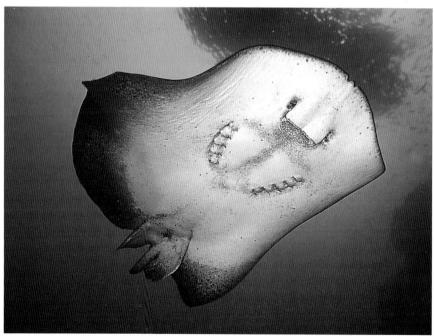

Blue-spotted ribbontail ray
Taeniura lymma (Forsskal, 1775)

101 △ ⬡ 🗺

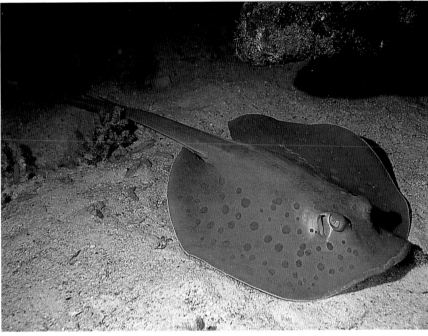

Family Dasyatidae
Range Limited to waters of tropical latitudes: Red Sea, Indian Ocean, western and central Pacific Ocean
Habitat Generally in shallow or very shallow water, tidal pools and in the intertidal zone, often on sandy beds of coral reefs. Rare or absent at a depth of more than 30 m (100 ft).
Size It grows to a length, including the tail, of 70 cm (27 in).
Habits Very common within its range and frequently sighted by divers and swimmers, although some-times the only part to be seen is the tail projecting from the coral formations: it is in fact not a species that buries itself in the sand. The disc is rounded, strongly raised near the head, with the back uni-

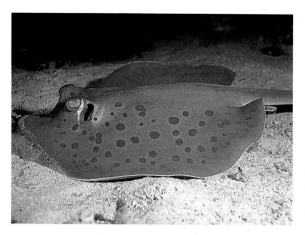

formly yellow or yellow-green and adorned with numerous circular spots of varying size, but always of a brilliant electric-blue. Two stripes of the same blue color run from the base of the tail to its tip. The belly is whitish, and the two huge, protuberant eyes on top of the head are bright yellow; and just behind the eye cavity is a prominent, broad spiracle. One or, more often, two serrated spines, connected to a poison-bearing gland, are located near the tip of the tail as a deterrent to predators, particularly sharks. Timid and as a rule content to lie motionless in a rock crevice, the ray, if alarmed, will make a sudden dash for freedom, zigzagging off through the corals at a truly astonishing rate.

This stingray feeds on small benthic fishes, mollusks and crustaceans, flushing them out from the substrate by rummaging through the sand and then rapidly chewing them up with the bony plates that serve as teeth. Thanks to the splendid coloration of the back—which undoubtedly makes it one of the most spectacular of the multicolored residents of the barrier reef—the blue-spotted ribbontail ray is one of the best-known species in the skin-diving community and a favorite subject for underwater photography.

Blue-spotted stingray
Dasyatis kuhlii (Muller & Henle, 1841)

102 △ ⋠

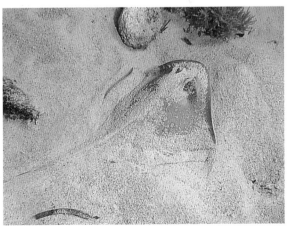

Family Dasyatidae
Range Confined to the tropical latitudes of the Indo-Pacific
Habitat Normally in shal-low and very shallow water, in tidal pools and in the intertidal zone, down to a depth of 60 m (200 ft). Common on sandy and muddy bottoms, some-times in estuaries and in brackish waters.

Size The total length, including the tail, may reach 40 cm (16 in).

Habits Quite common within its range but often not easily spotted by divers because of its habit of burying itself in the sand or mud, from which only the round, protuberant eyes are allowed to emerge. The sober, mimetic col-oration serves further to conceal its presence: the back is pale gray-green or gray-yellow, with a scatter-ing of variously sized bright blue ocelli, often bordered with black; the long, thin

tail is white at the tip.

In contrast to the species *Taeniura lymma* (see page 214)—similar but a typical resident of the coral reef—this species prefers sandy bottoms and turbid waters, sometimes frequenting mangroves and the brackish waters of estuaries. It, too, has one or more venomous spines on the tail, and if molested or threatened will wait motionless in the sand until the last moment and then make a sudden dash, swiftly changing direction to throw off its pursuer. It feeds on small benthic organisms such as gobies, shrimps, bivalves and other invertebrates, rummaging energetically in the sand to flush out hidden prey.

Southern stingray

Dasyatis americana (Hildebrand & Schroeder, 1928)

103 △ ⊄ ⊹

Family Dasyatidae
Range Tropical and sub-tropical waters of the western Atlantic Ocean from New Jersey to Brazil
Habitat Sandy sea floors, coastal lagoons, at a depth of not over 25 m (80 ft)
Size The average size range is 1.5–1.8 m (5–6 ft).
Habits The southern or American stingray is a large, powerful ray that frequents sandy seabeds of the Caribbean (it is the species that is found abundantly in the waters of Stingray City, a celebrated underwater diving site in the Cayman Islands). The back is lead-gray, brownish or uniformly olive, and

the belly is white; the underside of the long tail has a longitudinal skin-fold and a strong serrated spine at the juncture with the body. A row of spiny thorns lines the back. The eyes protrude, with the pupil protected by an extensible strip of skin that helps to camouflage the eye and at the same time regulate the amount of available light. Very conspicuous just behind the eye cavity is a large spiracle, often the only visible feature to betray the presence of the huge animal when buried in the sand.

The southern stingray is a shy, inquisitive, quite intelligent creature, capa-

ble of inflicting painful wounds with its caudal spine if disturbed or threatened: several cases have been reported of deaths caused by the stings of this and other large species such as the black-spotted stingray, *Taeniura melanospilos* (see page 212). The diet consists of shrimps, crabs, worms and small fish that it flushes out by night from the sandy sub-strate.

Family Dasyatidae
Range Red Sea, tropical western Indo-Pacific as far as Micronesia
Habitat Sandy and muddy beds of shallow coastal waters down to a depth of 42 m (140 ft), in atoll lagoons and also in the brackish waters of estuaries and mangrove swamps
Size It may grow to a width of 1.7 m (6 ft) and a length of 5 m (16 ft), including the very long tail.

The weight may exceed 118 kg (260 lbs).
Habits This is a very beautiful stingray of tropical seas, characterized by extremely variable colors. The ground is pale beige to brown, but always exhibiting the complex pattern of lighter wavy lines and small black spots. Another identifying feature when submerged is the long, slender, whiplike tail, though sometimes with the tip

missing as a result of an attack by a predator (usually a shark). It tends to be inactive during the day, often half-buried in the sandy bed with which it blends to perfection. Related species are the mangrove whipray, *Himantura granulata* (see page 223) and the leopard whipray, *H. undulata* (see page 221), with which it may easily be confused.

Family Dasyatidae
Range Tropical western Indo-Pacific
Habitat Sandy and muddy beds in coastal waters of the continental shelf, at depths of 3–80 m (10–260 ft), in atoll lagoons and also in the brackish waters of estuaries and mangrove swamps
Size It may grow to a width of 1.4 m (4.5 ft) and a length of about 5 m (16 ft), including the very long tail.

Habits This spectacular stingray of the Indo-Pacific is very similar to the honeycomb stingray, *Himantura uarnak* (see page 220), and is easily confused with the latter when submerged. Diagnostic features for identifying this species—normally inactive and half-buried in the sand—are the relatively more pointed disc and, above all, the extremely elegant leopard-like design with its black rosettes (no wavy lines) on a pale beige ground. Not especially common, the ray probably lives at greater depths than its relatives although it readily ventures into the shallows. It has one or more venomous spines situated about halfway down its tail.

Cowtail stingray
Pastinachus sephen (Forsskal, 1775)

△ ⬦

Family Dasyatidae
Range Tropical Indo-Pacfic, Red Sea
Habitat Sandy bottoms in coastal waters and on coral reefs in the open sea, down to a depth of 60 m (200 ft).
Size It grows to a length of 3 m (10 ft).

Habits A large ray typical of the family to which it belongs, with a very thick discoid body, uniformly brown on the back and white on the belly. The eyes are big and protruding, set close to the large spiracles. A characteristic feature for identifying the species is a broad ventral finfold along the tail, which makes the rear part look like a flag, particularly when the fish is swimming. The venomous spine is halfway down the tail. Fairly active, sometimes accompanied by remoras and pilotfish, it frequents the sandy spaces that intersperse the coral reef and the beds of estuaries and bays, partially covering itself with sand when at rest on the bottom, allowing only the eyes and spiracles to emerge. It feeds on crustaceans and mollusks that it digs out of the substrate.

Mangrove whipray

Himantura granulata (Macleay, 1883)

Family Dasyatidae

Range Tropical Indo-Pacific from Indonesia to northern Australia

Habitat An exclusively benthic species of sandy and detritic sea floors, sometimes in a few inches of water, along beaches and in mangrove forests

Size It grows to a width of 1.5 m (5 ft).

Habits A large whipray characterized, like all its relatives, by its broad, flat, rounded body, protuberant eyes set in a dorsal position and large, adjacent and clearly visible spiracles. The long tail is thin and flexible, whiplike and with one or more dangerous serrated spines. The color of the back is dark gray or brownish, with small white spots; the belly is white, speckled with black along the perimeter. The tail is almost invariably white or in any event lighter. During the day this stingray, too, normally remains on the bottom, often half-buried in the sand; at night it energetically hunts fish, crustaceans and bivalves in the substrate. Females give birth to live and perfectly formed young.

Porcupine ray
Urogymnus asperrimus (Bloch & Schneider, 1801)

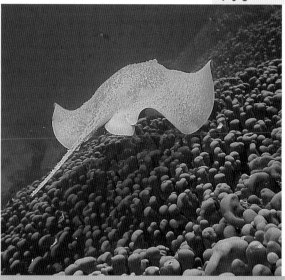

Family Dasyatidae
Range Tropical eastern Atlantic Ocean, tropical Indo-Pacific
Habitat Sandy and detritic sea floors and coral reefs
Size Up to 100 cm (39 in)
Habits Easily identifiable by its typically oval body, well rounded when seen from above, with a multitude of strong, variously sized thorns and pointed denticles. The coloration of the back is a very pale, uniform gray; the tail is short, sturdy, without poisonous spines.

Crossback stingaree
Urolophus cruciatus (Lacepède, 1804)

△

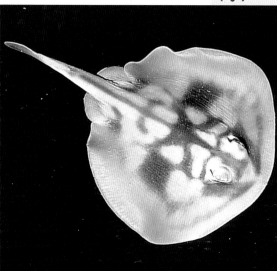

Family Urolophidae
Range Only in Australian waters, from New South Wales to Tasmania
Habitat Sandy, muddy or detritic bottoms in shallow water; also often around estuaries
Size Grows to a length of 50 cm (20 in).
Habits Nocturnal, normally half-buried in the substrate during the daytime. Innocuous, but able to inflict dangerous wounds with the tail spine if disturbed. The ray feeds on mollusks and small benthic crustaceans.

Pelagic stingray

Dasyatis (Pteroplatytrygon) violacea (Bonaparte, 1832)

Family Dasyatidae

Range Temperate and subtropical waters, worldwide

Habitat Exclusively pelagic, not at great depths, off the continental shelf

Size Up to a length of 1.6 m (5 ft) including tail, width up to 80 cm (31 in).

Habits An absolutely anomalous stingray, with an angular disc and a particularly long spine at the base of the tail. The eyes, in contrast to other rays, are not protuberant. The coloration is uniformly violet-gray or blue-green both on the back and the belly. It is a very rare species, wholly pelagic, seldom seen underwater and a very agile swimmer. It feeds in the main on pelagic crustaceans and small fishes, which it manipulates adroitly with the pectoral fins to drive them into the mouth. Sometimes caught accidentally by trawlers, its biology is scarcely known.

Sparsely-spotted stingaree
Urolophus paucimaculatus (Dixon, 1969)

||| △ ⌀✡

Family Urolophidae
Range Tropical western Pacific Ocean
Habitat Coastal waters, on sandy and muddy sea beds, down to a depth of 150 m (500 ft)
Size Grows up to 50 cm (20 in) long
Habits Known in Australia by the common name "stingarees," the small spotted stingrays belonging to the family Urolophidae are widely present in tropical and subtropical waters throughout the world. The tropical Indo-Pacific species are in general of small size, the short, muscular tail being armed with a single venomous spine: *Urolophus paucimaculatus* is distinguished from the related *U. cruciatus* (see page 224) by the less obvious cruciform design on the back and its wider distribution; *U. aurantiacus*, without any decorative motif on the back, is found from Japan to Vietnam and normally lives at greater depths. Fairly inactive, these small stingrays may represent a threat to swimmers because of their habit of lying motionless, half-buried in the sandy bottom.

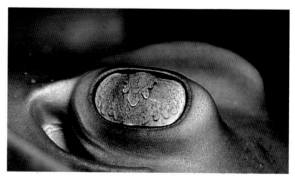

Yellow stingray
Urolophus jamaicensis (Cuvier, 1817)

112 △ ⟨⟩

Family Urolophidae
Range Tropical western Atlantic Ocean from North Carolina to Gulf of Mexico
Habitat Coastal waters, on sandy and muddy beds, down to a depth of 30 m (100 ft)
Size Up to a length of 50 cm (20 in)
Habits An elegant member of the family Urolophidae, its body splendidly patterned with a mixture of dark patches and spots on a yellowish ground, this species is also capable of changing, at will and with astonishing speed, the tonal depth of this distinctive design. *Urolophus jamaicensis* is a stingray of

medium dimensions, with a characteristically rounded disc and a muscular tail terminating in a prominent caudal fin. Relatively inactive during the daytime, it tends to ignore skin-divers, so that it is possible to get quite close while it is lying half-buried in the sand. If molested or inadvertently touched, however, it may lash out with its poisonous spine, located halfway down the tail, and cause painful wounds.

Banded stingray
Trygonoptera sp.

113 △ ⇭

Family Urolophidae
Range Almost exclusively in Australian waters, with an extremely localized dis-

tribution along the shores of southern New South Wales
Habitat All the species

classified in the genus *Trygonoptera* live on sandy and muddy bottoms of the intertidal zone down to 150 m (500 ft).
Size The maximum length is around 40 cm (16 in). Some species measure just over half a meter.
Habits The five species that belong to this genus are thus far little studied. As a rule, they feed on small crustaceans and benthic invertebrates; their range seems to be confined to Australian and Indonesian waters (*T. javanica*).

Round stingray
Urolophus halleri (Cooper, 1863)

114 △ ⇭

Family Urolophidae
Range From northern California to Panama
Habitat Sandy and muddy

bottoms, from the surface to a depth of 90 m (300 ft)
Size Adults grow to a

maximum length of just over 50 cm (20 in).
Habits Diurnal, often raised in captivity, this ray feeds on worms, crustaceans and invertebrates that it extracts from the substrate by digging characteristic holes, up to 13 cm (5 in) deep. Generally yellowish or brownish, with a smooth back, the specimen pictured here is seen eating the eggs of a squid that have just been laid on the bottom.

Bat ray
Myliobatis californicus (Gill, 1865)

115

Family Myliobatidae

Range Temperate eastern Pacific from Gulf of California to Oregon

Habitat Coastal waters, on sandy seabeds and in kelp forests to a depth of 20 m (65 ft)

Size It grows to 1.8 m (6 ft) wide.

Habits The eagle rays (Myliobatidae) are characterized by a large rhomboidal or quadrangular disc with a massive body and a large rounded snout that juts out at the front. The back is usually smooth, sometimes with small spiny tubercles down the middle. The tail is long and slender, shaped like a whip, armed with one to five venomous spines set close to the base. The coloration is dark gray, brown or greenish above and white underneath; the tips of the large pectoral fins are darker on the ventral surface. The various species alternate periods of activity—when they often swim in very big groups at medium depth or near the surface—with long periods of rest, during which they lie inactive on the bottom; if disturbed on such occasions, they first raise themselves on the pectoral fins and then accelerate suddenly and take off. The specimen illustrated in the photo-graph below is feeding on the newly laid eggs of a squid; the moment chosen by squid to breed along the Californian coasts attracts large numbers of predators, including rays and sharks, to the great delight of underwater photographers.

Family Myliobatidae

Range Tropical and subtropical waters worldwide

Habitat Surface waters down to a depth of 60 m (200 ft), close to the continental shelf. Often on stretches of sand at medium depth or on the bottom.

Size Presumably up to and over 3 m (10 ft) wide but as a rule 1.6–2 m (5–6.5 ft)

Habits This species is a graceful swimmer and very elegant, its back handsomely patterned with light-colored spots and rosettes densely packed on a blue-gray or dark green ground. The belly is white and the tail, long and thin, is equipped with one or more serrated spines that get smaller toward the base. The body is rhomboidal, with large triangular pectoral fins similar to wings.

Another identifying feature is the unusual, projecting "duck-billed" mouth, with which the ray rakes the sandy bottom, methodi-

cally digging out the small benthic fishes, crustaceans and mollusks that it rapidly devours with its strong, bony platelike teeth.

The eagle rays are highly active, generally gregarious (in groups ranging from three to over a hundred individuals). Although they normally swim slowly and sedately, they can accelerate at astonishing speed to escape natural enemies such as sharks (whose curved bites may often be seen on the rear edge of the pectorals of larger specimens) and skindivers, with whom, unfortunately, they avoid con-

tact. They are, in fact, very shy and among the most difficult animals to approach underwater, so that a good photograph of an eagle ray is considered a prized trophy. Sometimes they will leap out of the water, presumably to get rid of irritating skin

parasites. This species performs complex and spectacular courtship rituals, and the females, after a gestation period of 12 months, give birth to 1–4 live, perfectly formed young.

Pacific cownose ray

Rhinoptera steindachneri (Evermann & Jenkins, 1892)

Family Rhinopteridae
Range Tropical eastern Pacific from Baja California to Peru, including the Galapagos
Habitat Coastal waters, in bays and estuaries and on sandy and muddy sea floors, often close to mangrove swamps
Size Up to 1.5 m (5 ft) wide.
Habits A powerful ray with a very thick body and a lozenge-shaped disc, with a thin whiplike tail and a head quite distinct from the trunk. The forehead is distinctly bilobate, with a broad, concave snout and clearly visible, laterally positioned eyes. The back is uniformly dark gray or brownish, and the belly is white. It is an active species of characteristic and almost unmistakable appearance, sometimes assembling in large groups (up to a thousand individuals); it swims slowly and gracefully but is extremely shy and very difficult to approach underwater. Food consists of small fishes, crustaceans and bivalves that it flushes from the substrate and chews up with the bony plates that make up its powerful dentition. Virtually identical to it is the related *Rhinoptera javanica*, whose range extends from Africa to Indonesia. The females give birth to 1–6 live young.

Family Rhinopteridae

Range Tropical and subtropical Atlantic Ocean from Massachusetts to Brazil

Habitat Coastal waters, in bays and estuaries and on sandy and muddy sea floors, often close to mangrove swamps.

Size Up to 1.5 m (5 ft) wide

Habits A powerful ray with a thick body and lozenge-shaped disc, a short, thin tail and head quite distinct from the trunk. This species, too, is absolutely unmistakable and easy to identify at first glance. The forehead is markedly bilobate, with a broad, concave snout and very visible eyes. The back is uniformly gray or brown, the belly is white. An acive species, it is a slow, elegant swimmer but extremely timid and thus hard to approach underwater. Its diet comprises small fishes, crus- taceans and bivalves that it strains from the substrate and consumes with its strong, bony platelike teeth. Substantially similar to the related species *Rhinoptera javanica* and *R. steindachneri* (see page 232). The females give birth to 1–6 live young.

Manta ray
Manta birostris (Donndorff, 1798)

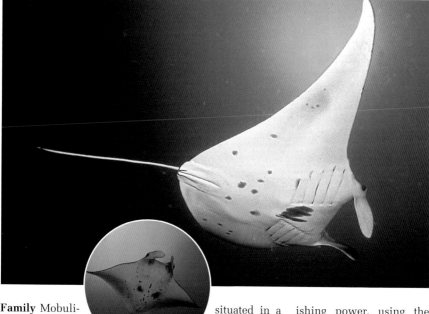

Family Mobulidae
Range Tropical waters worldwide
Habitat Pelagic, but often sighted near coasts, presumably as a result of seasonal migrations: from the surface down to a maximum depth of 40 m (135 ft)
Size Presumably up to 9 m (30 ft) wide, but generally 3–5 m (10–16 ft). The weight may exceed 1,000 kg (2,200 lbs). However, individuals of gigantic proportions, once frequent, are now very rare.
Habits It is the biggest of the rays, with broad pectoral fins comparable to wings, an enormous mouth, no teeth, situated in a terminal position (not ventral, as with other rays), and the presence of so-called cephalic lobes, i.e., modified, spoon-shaped extensions of the pectoral fins. The tail is short, very slender and without spines. The color of the back is gray-blue or black, often with paler symmetrical patches, and the belly is white, frequently with darker markings; and certain specimens are melanistic—dark all over.

Solitary or in small groups of up to 15 or so individuals, it swims with great elegance yet astonishing power, using the large cephalic lobes (which curl back on themselves during high-speed swimming) to drive the plankton on which it feeds into its open mouth. Here the minuscule pelagic organisms are drawn in by the modified gill arches, and the water used for breathing is normally expelled through the large gill slits located on the underside.

Harmless to humans, if not threatened it will often show marked curiosity toward skin-divers and may keep them company for some time, even performing spectacular under-

water acrobatics; for its part, it is frequently accompanied by remoras and pilotfish. The female gives birth to 1–2 live young, about 120 cm (47 in) wide and weighing 45 kg (100 lbs), while leaping into the air.

Relatively common within its range, this majestic species is regularly caught in many areas—especially in Mexican waters and in the Gulf of California—for the food and craft industries, and must therefore be considered seriously endangered.

Devil ray
Mobula sp. (Cuvier, 1829)

Family Mobulidae
Range Essentially in tropical waters worldwide
Habitat Pelagic and in coastal waters, on sandy beds and coral reefs in the open sea, to a depth of 20 m (65 ft)
Size Adults may grow to a length of 1.2 m (4 ft).
Habits The various species known generically as devil rays or devil fishes are all of similar appearance, sometimes furnished with small venomous spines situated at the base of the tail. Outwardly, in fact,

they appear almost identical to a small manta (the head is proportionally bigger) and their habits, too, are very similar: but these more modest species tend to move about in groups and are seldom encountered on their own. They are all highly active animals, excellent swimmers that feed on plankton, and have a preference for stretches of ocean traversed by strong currents. Among the most common species in tropical waters of the Indo-Pacific are *Mobula japanica* (the largest of all), *M. thurstoni* (characterized by the concave forward edge of the disc) and *M. eregoodootenkee.*

Rabbitfish

Chimaera monstrosa (Linnaeus, 1758)

121

Habits Certainly the best known of the so-called short-nosed chimaeras, this species has a large rounded snout and big eyes, indications of a life spent at very great depths. Despite being inhabitants of the abyss, the chimaeras of the genera *Hydrolagus* and *Chimaera* are occasionally sighted in shallower waters (the photograph of the specimen illustrated here was taken in a Norwegian fiord).

Family Chimaeridae
Range Atlantic Ocean from North Sea to Azores, and Mediterranean

Habitat Ocean depths down to at least 1,000 m (3,280 ft).
Size Up to 80 cm (31 in)

Spotted ratfish

Hydrolagus colliei (Lay & Bennett, 1839)

122

(1,400–2,500 ft)
Size Up to a length of 96 cm (38 in)
Habits The chimaeras are grouped in three families, numbering at least 31 species. All are characterized by a cartilaginous skeleton, a spiny, erectile first dorsal fin, smooth skin, big eyes, ventrally placed mouth and a single pair of gill slits. The ratfish, *Hydrolagus colliei*, has a scattering of white spots the length of its body.

Family Chimaeridae
Range Eastern Pacific Ocean from Alaska to Baja California

Habitat At depths of 9–965 m (30–3,200 ft); generally on abyssal seabeds at depths of 420–750 m

Long-nosed chimaera
Harriotta raleighana (Goode & Bean, 1895)

123

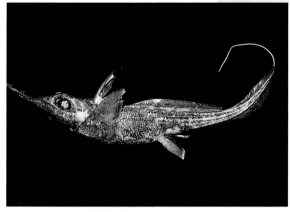

Habits A chimaera characterized, as the name of the family suggests, by a strikingly long, flattened snout. The coloration is blackish or uniformly brown: the caudal fin terminates in a long filament. This is a rare species and almost nothing is known about its biology and habits.

Family Rhinochimaeridae
Range Atlantic and Pacific Oceans
Habitat Abyssal waters at depths of 850–1,100 m (2,800–3,600 ft)
Size Up to 100 cm (39 in) in length

Elephant fish
Callorhinchus milii (Bory de Saint-Vincent, 1823)

124

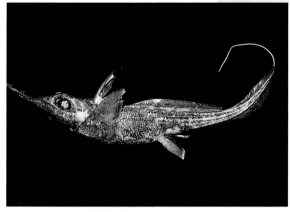

Size Presumably to more than 1.2 m (4 ft) in length
Habit The chimaeras of this family are silver in color, with a body flattened from side to side, with a strange trunklike projection at the tip of the snout. The family contains two species, at least one of which (*Callorhinchus capensis*) is regularly fished for edible purposes in southern African waters. Unlike other species of chimaeras, it may sometimes be sighted in coastal waters and at moderate depth.

Family Callorhinchidae
Range Southern Australia, Tasmania and New Zealand
Habitat From the shallow coastal waters of the continental shelf to a depth of 200 m (660 ft)

APPENDICES

CLASSIFICATION OF SHARKS

By Leonard J.V. Compagno, FAO, 1984

HEXANCHIFORMES

CHLAMYDOSELACHIDAE

•*Chlamydoselachus*
C. anguineus (Garman, 1884)

HEXANCHIDAE

•*Heptranchias*
H. perlo (Bonnaterre, 1788)
•*Hexanchus*
H. griseus (Bonnaterre, 1788)
H. vitulus (Springer & Waller)
•*Notorynchus*
N. cepedianus (Peron, 1807)

SQUALIFORMES

ECHINORHINIDAE

•*Echinorhinus*
E. brucus (Bonnaterre, 1788)
E. cookei (Pietschmann, 1928)

SQUALIDAE

•*Aculeola*
A. nigra (De Buen, 1959
•*Centrophorus*
C. acus (Garman, 1906)
C. granulosus (Bloch & Schneider, 1801)
C. harrissoni (McCulloch, 1915)
C. lustianicus (Bocage & Capello, 1864)
C. moluccensis (Bleeker, 1860)
C. niaukang (Teng, 1959)
C. squamosus (Bonnaterre, 1788)
C. tessellatus (Garman, 1906)
C. uyato (Rafinesque, 1810)
•*Centroscyllium*
C. fabricii (Reinhardt, 1825)
C. granulatum (Gunther, 1887)
C. kamoharai (Abe, 1966)
C. nigrum (Garman, 1899)
C. ornatum (Alcock, 1889)
C. ritteri (Jordan & Fowler, 1903)
•*Centroscymnus*
C. coelolepis (Bocage & Capello, 1864)
C. crepidater (Bocage & Capello, 1864)
C. cryptacanthus (Regan, 1906)
C. macracanthus (Regan, 1906)
C. owstoni (Garman, 1906)
C. plunketi (Waite, 1900)

- *Cirrhigaleus*
C. *barbifer* (Tanaka, 1912)
- *Dalatias*
D. *licha* (Bonnaterre, 1788)
- *Deania*
D. *calcea* (Lowe, 1839)
D. *histricosa* (Garman, 1906)
D. *profundorum* (Smith & Radcliffe, 1912)
D. *quadrispinosum* (McCulloch, 1915)
- *Etmopterus*
E. *baxteri* (Garrick, 1957)
E. *brachyurus* (Smith & Radcliffe, 1912)
E. *bullisi* (Bigelow & Schroeder, 1957)
E. *decacuspidatus* (Chan, 1966)
E. *gracilispinis* (Krefft, 1968)
E. *granulosus* (Gunther, 1880)
E. *hillianus* (Poey, 1861)
E. *lucifer* (Jordan & Snyder, 1902)
E. *polli* (Bigelow, Schroeder & Springer, 1953)
E. *princeps* (Collett, 1904)
E. *pusillus* (Lowe, 1839)
E. *schultzi* (Bigelow, Schroeder & Springer, 1953)
E. *spinax* (Linnaeus, 1758)
E. *unicolor* (Engelhardt, 1912)
E. *villosus* (Gilbert, 1905)
E. *virens* (Bigelow, Schroeder & Springer, 1953)
- *Euprotomicroides*
E. *zantedeschia* (Hulley & Penrith, 1966)
- *Euprotomicrus*
E. *bispinatus* (Quoy & Gaimard, 1824)
- *Heteroscymnoides*
H. *marleyi* (Fowler, 1934)
- *Isistius*
I. *brasiliensis* (Quoy & Gaimard, 1824)
I. *plutodus* (Garrick & Springer, 1964)
- *Scymnodalatias*
S. *sherwoodi* (Archey, 1921)
- *Scymnodon*
S. *obscurus* (Vaillant, 1888)
S. *ringens* (Bocage & Capello)
S. *squamulosus* (Gunther, 1877)
- *Somniosus*
S. *microcephalus* (Bloch & Schneider, 1801)
S. *pacificus* (Bigelow & Schroeder, 1944)
S. *rostratus* (Risso, 1826)
- *Squaliolus*
S. *laticaudus* (Smith & Radcliffe, 1912)
- *Squalus*
S. *acanthias* (Smith & Radcliffe, 1912)
S. *asper* (Merrett, 1973)
S. *blainvillei* (Risso, 1826)
S. *cubensis* (Howell-Rivero, 1936)
S. *japonicus* (Ishikawa, 1908)

S. *megalops* (Macleay, 1881)
S. *melanurus* (Fourmanoir & Rivaton, 1979)
S. *mitsukurii* (Jordan & Snyder, 1903)
S. *rancureli* (Fourmanoir & Rivaton, 1979)

OXYNOTIDAE

- *Oxynotus*
O. *bruniensis* (Ogilby, 1893)
O. *caribbaeus* (Cervigon, 1961)
O. *centrina* (Linnaeus, 1758)
O. *paradoxus* (Frade, 1929)

PRISTIOPHORIFORMES

PRISTIOPHORIDAE

- *Pliotrema*
P. *warreni* (Regan, 1906)
- *Pristiophorus*
P. *cirratus* (Latham, 1794)
P. *japonicus* (Gunther, 1870)
P. *nudipinnis* (Gunther, 1870)
P. *schroederi* (Springer & Bullis, 1960)

SQUATINIFORMES

SQUATINIDAE

- *Squatina*
S. *aculeata* (Dumeril, 1829)
S. *africana* (Regan, 1908)
S. *argentina* (Marini, 1930)
S. *australis* (Regan, 1906)
S. *californica* (Ayres, 1859)
S. *dumeril* (Le Sueur, 1818)
S. *formosa* (Shen & Ting, 1972)
S. *japonica* (Bleeker, 1858)
S. *nebulosa* (Regan, 1906)
S. *oculata* (Bonaparte, 1840)
S. *squatina* (Linnaeus, 1758)
S. *tergocellata* (McCulloch, 1914)
S. *tergocellatoides* (Chen, 1963)

HETERODONTIFORMES

HETERODONTIDAE

- *Heterodontus*
H. *francisci* (Girard, 1854)
H. *galeatus* (Gunther, 1870)
H. *japonicus* (Maclay & Macleay, 1884)
H. *mexicanus* (Taylor & Castro-Aguirre, 1972)

H. portusjacksoni (Meyer, 1793)
H. quoyi (Freminville, 1840)
H. ramalheira (Smith, 1949)
H. zebra (Gray, 1831)

ORECTOLOBIFORMES

PARASCYLLIDAE

•*Cirrhoscyllium*
C. formosanum (Teng, 1959)
C. japonicum (Kamohara, 1943)
•*Parascyllium*
P. collare (Ramsay & Ogilby, 1888)
P. ferrugineum (McCulloch, 1911)
P. multimaculatum (Scott, 1935)
P. variolatum (Dumeril, 1853)

BRACHAELURIDAE

•*Brachaelurus*
B. waddi (Bloch & Schneider, 1801)
•*Heteroscyllium*
H. colcloughi (Ogilby, 1908)

ORECTOLOBIDAE

•*Eucrossorhinus*
E. dasypogon (Bleeker, 1867)
•*Orectolobus*
O. japonicus (Regan, 1906)
O. maculatus (Bonnaterre, 1788)
O. ornatus (de Vis, 1883)
•*Sutorectus*
S. tentaculatus (Peters, 1864)

HEMISCYLLIIDAE

•*Chiloscyllium*
C. caerulopunctatum (Pellegrin, 1914)
C. griseum (Muller & Henle, 1838)
C. indicum (Gmelin, 1789)
C. plagiosum (Bennett, 1830)
C. punctatum (Muller & Henle, 1838)
•*Hemiscyllium*
H. freycineti (Quoy & Gaimard, 1824)
H. hallstromi (Whitley, 1967)
H. ocellatum (Bonnaterre, 1788)
H. strahani (Whitley, 1967)
H. trispeculare (Richardson, 1843)

STEGOSTOMATIDAE

•*Stegostoma*
S. fasciatum (Hermann, 1783)

GINGLYMOSTOMATIDAE

•*Ginglymostoma*
G. cirratum (Bonnaterre, 1788)
•*Nebrius*
N. ferrugineus (Lesson, 1830)

RHINIODONTIDAE

•*Rhiniodon*
R. typus (Smith, 1828)

LAMNIFORMES

ODONTASPIDIDAE

•*Eugomphodus*
E. taurus (Rafinesque, 1810)
E. tricuspidatus (Day, 1878)
•*Odontaspis*
O. ferox (Risso, 1810)
O. noronhai (Maul, 1955)

MITSUKURINIDAE

•*Mitsukurina*
M. owstoni (Jordan, 1898)

PSEUDOCARCHARIIDAE

•*Pseudocarcharias*
P. kamoharai (Matsubara, 1936)

MEGACHASMIDAE

•*Megachasma*
M. pelagios (Taylor, Compagno & Struhsaker, 1983)

ALOPIIDAE

•*Alopias*
A. pelagicus (Nakamura, 1935)
A. superciliosus (Lowe, 1839)
A. vulpinus (Bonnaterre, 1788)

CETORHINIDAE

•*Cetorhinus*
C. maximus (Gunnerus, 1745)

LAMNIDAE

•*Carcharodon*
C. carcharias (Linnaeus, 1758)

Isurus
I. oxyrinchus (Rafinesque, 1809)
I. paucus (Guitart Manday, 1966)
•Lamna
L. ditropis (Hubbs & Follett, 1947)
L. nasus (Bonnaterre, 1788)

CARCHARHINIFORMES

SCYLIORHINIDAE

•Apristurus
A. atlanticus (Koefoed, 1932)
A. brunneus (Gilbert, 1892)
A. canutus (Springer & Heemstra, 1979)
A. herklotsi (Fowler, 1934)
A. indicus (Brauer, 1906)
A. investigatoris (Misra, 1962)
A. japonicus (Nakaya, 1975)
A. kampae (Taylor, 1972)
A. laurussoni (Saemundsson, 1922)
A. longicephalus (Nakaya, 1975)
A. macrorhynchus (Tanaka, 1909)
A. maderensis (Cadenat & Maul, 1966)
A. manis (Springer, 1979)
A. microps (Gilchrist, 1922)
A. nasutus (de Buen, 1959)
A. parvipinnis (Springer & Heemstra, 1979)
A. platyrhynchus (Tanaka, 1909)
A. profundorum (Goode & Bean, 1896)
A. riveri (Bigelow & Schroeder, 1944)
A. saldanha (Barnard, 1925)
A. sibogae (Weber, 1913)
A. sinensis (Chu & Hu, 1981)
A. spongiceps (Gilbert, 1895)
A. stenseni (Springer, 1979)
A. verweyi (Fowler, 1934)
•Asymbolus
A. analis (Ogilby, 1885)
A. vincenti (Zeitz, 1908)
•Atelomycterus
A. macleayi (Whitley, 1939)
A. marmoratus (Bennett, 1830)
•Aulohalaelurus
A. labiosus (Waite, 1905)
•Cephaloscyllium
C. fasciatum (Chan, 1966)
C. isabellum (Bonnaterre, 1788)
C. laticeps (Dumeril, 1853)
C. nascione (Whitley, 1932)
C. silasi (Talwar, 1974)
C. sufflans (Regan, 1921)
C. ventriosum (Garman, 1880)
•Cephalurus

C. cephalus (Gilbert, 1892)
•Galeus
G. arae (Nichols, 1927)
G. boardmani (Whitley, 1928)
G. eastmani (Jordan & Snyder, 1904)
G. melastomus (Rafinesque, 1810)
G. murinus (Collett, 1904)
G. nipponensis (Nakaya, 1975)
G. piperatus (Springer & Wagner, 1966)
G. polli (Cadenat, 1959)
G. sauteri (Jordan & Richardson, 1909)
G. schultzi (Springer, 1979)
•Halaelurus
H. alcocki (Garman, 1913)
H. boesemani (Springer & D'Aubrey, 1972)
H. buergeri (Muller & Henle, 1838)
H. canescens (Gunther, 1878)
H. dawsoni (Springer, 1971)
H. hispidus (Alcock, 1891)
H. immaculatus (Chu & Meng, 1982)
H. lineatus (Bass, D'Aubrey & Kistnasamy, 1975)
H. lutarius (Springer & D'Aubrey, 1972)
H. natalensis (Regan, 1904)
H. quagga (Alcock, 1899)
•Haploblepharus
H. edwardsii (Voigt, 1832)
H. fuscus (Smith, 1950)
H. pictus (Muller & Henle, 1838)
•Holohalaelurus
H. punctatus (Gilchrist, 1914)
H. regani (Gilchrist, 1922)
•Parmaturus
P. campechiensis (Springer, 1979)
P. melanobranchius (Chan, 1966)
P. pilosus (Garman, 1906)
P. xaniurus (Gilbert, 1892)
•Pentanchus
P. profundicolus (Smith & Radcliffe, 1912)
•Poroderma
P. africanum (Gmelin, 1789)
P. marleyi (Fowler, 1934)
P. pantherinum (Smith, 1838)
•Schroederichthys
S. bivius (Smith, 1838)
S. chilensis (Guichenot, 1848)
S. maculatus (Springer, 1966)
S. tenuis (Springer, 1966)
•Scyliorhinus
S. besnardi (Springer & Sadowsky, 1970)
S. boa (Goode & Bean, 1896)
S. canicula (Linnaeus, 1758)
S. capensis (Smith, 1838)
S. cervigoni (Maurin & Bonnet, 1970)
S. garmani (Fowler, 1934)

S. *haeckeli* (Ribeiro, 1907)
S. *hesperius* (Springer, 1966)
S. *meadi* (Springer, 1966)
S. *retifer* (Garman, 1881)
S. *stellaris* (Linnaeus, 1758)
S. *torazame* (Tanaka, 1908)
S. *torrei* (Howell-Rivero, 1936)

PROSCYLLIIDAE

•*Ctenacis*
C. *fehlmanni* (Springer, 1968)
•*Eridacnis*
E. *barbouri* (Bigelow & Schroeder, 1944)
E. *radcliffei* (Smith, 1913)
E. *sinuans* (Smith, 1957)
•*Gollum*
G. *attenuatus* (Garrick, 1954)
•*Proscyllium*
P. *habereri* (Hilgendorf, 1904)

PSEUDOTRIAKIDAE

•*Pseudotriakis*
P. *microdon* (Capello, 1868)

LEPTOCHARIIDAE

•*Leptocharias*
L. *smithii* (Muller & Henle, 1839)

TRIAKIDAE

•*Furgaleus*
F. *macki* (Whitley, 1943)
•*Galeorhinus*
G. *galeus* (Linnaeus, 1758)
•*Gogolia*
G. *filewoodi* (Compagno, 1973)
•*Hemitriakis*
H. *japanica* (Muller & Henle, 1839)
H. *leucoperiptera* (Herre, 1923)
•*Hypogaleus*
H. *hyugaensis* (Miyosi, 1939)
•*Iago*
I. *garricki* (Fourmanoir & Rivaton, 1979)
I. *omanensis* (Norman, 1939)
•*Mustelus*
M. *antarcticus* (Gunther, 1870)
M. *asterias* (Cloquet, 1821)
M. *californicus* (Gill, 1864)
M. *canis* (Mitchell, 1815)
M. *dorsalis* (Gill, 1864)

M. *fasciatus* (Garman, 1913)
M. *griseus* (Pietschmann, 1908)
M. *henlei* (Gill, 1863)
M. *higmani* (Springer & Lowe, 1963)
M. *lenticulatus* (Phillipps, 1932)
M. *lunulatus* (Jordan & Gilbert, 1883)
M. *manazo* (Bleeker, 1854)
M. *mento* (Cope, 1877)
M. *mosis* (Hemprich & Ehrenberg, 1899)
M. *mustelus* (Linnaeus, 1758)
M. *norrisi* (Springer, 1940)
M. *palumbes* (Smith, 1957)
M. *punctulatus* (Risso, 1826)
M. *schmitti* (Springer, 1940)
M. *whitneyi* (Chirichigno, 1973)
•*Scylliogaleus*
S. *quecketti* (Boulenger, 1902)
•*Triakis*
T. *acutipinna* (Kato, 1968)
T. *maculata* (Kner & Steindachner, 1866)
T. *megalopterus* (Smith, 1849)
T. *scyllium* (Muller & Henle, 1839)
T. *semifasciata* (Girard, 1854)

HEMIGALEIDAE

•*Chaenogaleus*
C. *macrostoma* (Bleeker, 1852)
•*Hemigaleus*
H. *microstoma* (Bleeker, 1852)
•*Hemipristis*
H. *elongatus* (Klunzinger, 1871)
•*Paragaleus*
P. *pectoralis* (Garman, 1906)
P. *tengi* (Chen, 1963)

CARCHARHINIDAE

•*Carcharhinus*
C. *acronotus* (Poey, 1860)
C. *albimarginatus* (Ruppell, 1837)
C. *altimus* (Springer, 1950)
C. *amblyrhynchoides* (Whitley, 1934)
C. *amblyrhynchos* (Bleeker, 1856)
C. *amboinensis* (Muller & Henle, 1839)
C. *borneensis* (Bleeker, 1859)
C. *brachyurus* (Gunther, 1870)
C. *brevipinna* (Muller & Henle, 1839)
C. *cautus* (Whitley, 1945)
C. *dussumieri* (Valenciennes, 1839)
C. *falciformis* (Bibron, 1839)
C. *fitzroyensis* (Whitley, 1943)
C. *galapagensis* (Snodgrass & Heller, 1905)

C. *hemiodon* (Valenciennes, 1839)
C. *isodon* (Valenciennes, 1839)
C. *leucas* (Valenciennes, 1839)
C. *limbatus* (Valenciennes, 1839)
C. *longimanus* (Poey, 1861)
C. *macloti* (Muller & Henle, 1839)
C. *melanopterus* (Quoy & Gaimard, 1824)
C. *obscurus* (Le Sueur, 1818)
C. *perezi* (Poey, 1876)
C. *plumbeus* (Nardo, 1827)
C. *porosus* (Ranzani, 1839)
C. *sealei* (Pietschmann, 1916)
C. *signatus* (Poey, 1868)
C. *sorrah* (Valenciennes, 1839)
C. *wheeleri* (Garrick, 1982)
•*Galeocerdo*
G. *cuvier* (Peron & Le Sueur, 1822)
•*Glyphis*
G. *gangeticus* (Muller & Henle, 1839)
G. *glyphis* (Muller & Henle, 1839)
•*Isogomphodon*
I. *oxyrhynchus* (Muller & Henle, 1839)
•*Lamiopsis*
L. *temmincki* (Muller & Henle, 1839)
•*Loxodon*
L. *macrorhinus* (Muller & Henle, 1839)
•*Nasolamia*
N. *velox* (Gilbert, 1898)
•*Negaprion*
N. *acutidens* (Ruppell, 1837)

N. *brevirostris* (Poey, 1868)
•*Prionace*
P. *glauca* (Linnaeus, 1758)
•*Rhizoprionodon*
R. *acutus* (Ruppell, 1837)
R. *lalandii* (Valenciennes, 1839)
R. *longurio* (Jordan & Gilbert, 1882)
R. *oligolinx* (Springer, 1964)
R. *porosus* (Poey, 1861)
R. *taylori* (Ogilby, 1915)
R. *terraenovae* (Richardson, 1836)
•*Scoliodon*
S. *laticaudus* (Muller & Henle, 1838)
•*Triaenodon*
T. *obesus* (Ruppell, 1837)

SPHYRNIDAE

•*Eusphyra*
E. *blochii* (Cuvier, 1871)
•*Sphyrna*
S. *corona* (Springer, 1940)
S. *couardi* (Cadenat, 1950)
S. *lewini* (Griffith & Smith, 1834)
S. *media* (Springer, 1940)
S. *mokarran* (Ruppell, 1837)
S. *tiburo* (Linnaeus, 1758)
S. *tudes* (Valenciennes, 1822)
S. *zygaena* (Linnaeus, 1758)

Numbers in **bold** refer to main text entries, roman to text references, *italics* to illustration pages.

INDEX

The Shark: Splendid Savage of the Sea
Jacques-Yves Cousteau and Phillippe Cousteau, New York: Doubleday and Company, Inc., 1970

Killers of the Seas
Edward Ricciuti, New York: Walker and Company, 1973

The Natural History of Sharks
Thomas H. Lineaweaver III and Richard H. Backus, New York: J.B. Lippincott Co., 1970

FAO Species Cataglogue, Vol. 4. Sharks of the World. An Annotated and Illustrated Catalogue of Shark Species Known to Date
L.J V. Compagno, FAO, 1984

Sharks of Arabia
John E. Randall, London: Immel Publishing, 1986

Squali
Various authors, Rizzoli, 1987

Guide to the Sharks and Rays of Southern Africa
J.L.V. Compagno, Dave Ebert, Cape Town: Struik Publishers, 1989

Sharks and Rays of the Pacific Coast
Ava Ferguson and Gregor Cailliet, California: Monterey Bay Aquarium, 1990

Diver's Guide to the Sharks of the Maldives
R.C. Anderson, Novelty Publications, 1992

The Great White Shark
Jean-Michel Cousteau and Mose Richards, New York: Harry N. Abrams, 1992

Sharks of the World
Rodney Steel, London: Blandford, 1992

Shark: A Photographer's Story
Jeremy Stafford-Deitsch, Sierra Club Books, 1987

Reef Sharks and Rays of the World
Scott W. Michael, Monterey, California Sea Challengers, 1993

Sharks of Hawaii—Their Biology and Cultural Significance
Leighton Taylor, Honolulu: University of Hawaii Press, 1993

Sharks and Rays of Australia
P.R. Last and J.D. Stevens, East Melbourne CSIRO Information Services, 1993

Southeast Asia Tropical Fish Guide
Rudie H. Kuiter and Helmut Debelius, Germany: IKAN-Unterwasserarchiv, 1994

Sharks: Myth and Reality
Gaetano Cafiero and Maddalena Jahoda, White Star, 1994

Sharks
Doug Perrine, Stillwater, MN: Voyageur Press, 1995

Shark: Endangered Predator of the Sea
Marty Snyderman, Toronto: Key Porter Books, 1995

Sharks of Tropical and Temperate Seas
R.H. Johnson, Pisces Books, 1995

Shadows in the Sea: the Sharks, Skates and Rays
Thomas B. Allen, H.W. McCormick, and W.E. Young, The Lyons Press, 1996

Squali
Piero Angela, Mondadori, 1997

Sharks: History and Biology of the Lords of the Sea
Angelo Mojetta, Thunder Bay Press, 1999

Gli squali
Various authors, De Agostini, 1998

Sharks and Rays of the World
Doug Perrine, Stillwater, MN: Voyageur Press, 1999

SURFING THE INTERNET TO DISCOVER THE WORLD OF SHARKS

A number of websites deal with the subject of sharks and, more generally, Elasmobranchii, set up by private and governmental research organizations and by enthusiasts. The following list gives some of the more interesting ones, all of them providing information and further suggestions for those wishing to go into the subject in greater depth.

Einst Waren Wir Herrscher
http://www.elasmo.de/

Zoological Parks Board of New South Wales
http://www.zoo.nsw.gov.au/

Natal Sharks Board
http://shark.co.za/right.htm

Apex Predators Program
http://www.na.nmfs.gov /sharks/

The Whale Shark Bibliography
http://scilib.ucsd.edu/sio /indexes/whalshrk.html

Classification of the Recent Elasmobranchii
http://vsb.life.nottingham.ac .uk/elasmobranch/sharkray1 .htm

The Tricas Elasmobiology Lab
http://www.fit.edu/AcadRes /biology/tricas/lab-main.htm

Mote Marine Laboratory
http://www.mote.org/

The American Elasmobranch Society
http://www.elasmo.org

National Geographic
http://www .nationalgeographic.com /features/97/sharks

Fiona's Shark Mania
http://www.oceanstar.com /shark/

The Pelagic Shark Research Foundation
http://www.pelagic.org /index.html

Ichthyology at the Florida Museum of Natural History
http://www.flmnh.ufl.edu /fish/sharks/sharks.htm

Study Shark Biology
http://www.mote.org /~rhueter/sharkcrs.phtml

A Masterpiece of Evolution— The Shark
http://www.ncf.carleton.ca /~bz050/HomePage.shark.html

Shark Foundation
http://www.shark.ch

Clash of the Titans: Whale vs. Shark
http://www.cnn.com/EARTH /9710/08/whale.vs.shark/

Sharks: Research/ Informational Sites
http://edtech.kennesaw.edu /web/sharks.htm

Mediterranean Shark Site
http://www.zoo.co.uk /~z9015043/

1. Andrea and Antonella Ferrari
2-3. Andrea and Antonella Ferrari
4-5. Marty Snyderman/Innerspace Visions
6-7. Doug Perrine/Innerspace Visions
9. Doug Perrine/Innerspace Visions
10-11. Andrea and Antonella Ferrari
12. Andrea and Antonella Ferrari
13. Mark Strickland/Innerspace Visions
14. above Andrea and Antonella Ferrari
14. below Ben Cropp/Innerspace Visions
15. all Andrea and Antonella Ferrari
16. all Andrea and Antonella Ferrari
17. above Andrea and Antonella Ferrari
17. below Antonio Busetto
18. all Andrea and Antonella Ferrari
19. above Doug Perrine/Innerspace Visions
19. below Andrea and Antonella Ferrari
20. above Piero Cozzaglio
20. below John G. Maiser/American Museum of Natural History
21. R. Crespi
22. above John G. Maiser/American Museum of Natural History
22. below Piero Cozzaglio
23. above and right Andrea and Antonella Ferrari
23. below John G. Maiser/American Museum of Natural History
24. all Andrea and Antonella Ferrari
25. above Andrea and Antonella Ferrari
25. below right Mark Conlin/Innerspace Vision
25. others right Doug Perrine/Innerspace Visions
26. above left Mark Strickland/Innerspace Visions
26. others left Doug Perrine/Innerspace Visions
26. below Andrea and Antonella Ferrari
27. all Doug Perrine/Innerspace Visions
28. above Andrea and Antonella Ferrari
28. below Ben Cropp/Innerspace Visions
29. all Andrea and Antonella Ferrari
30. all Andrea and Antonella Ferrari
31. all Andrea and Antonella Ferrari
32. Andrea and Antonella Ferrari
33. Rory McGinnis
34. Ron and Valerie Taylor
35. Ron and Valerie Taylor
36. Andrea and Antonella Ferrari
37. Doug Perrine/Innerspace Visions
38. all Andrea and Antonella Ferrari
39. above Doug Perrine/Innerspace Visions
39. right Andrea and Antonella Ferrari
40. all Andrea and Antonella Ferrari
41. above Andrea and Antonella Ferrari
41. below Doug Perrine/Innerspace Visions
42. all Andrea and Antonella Ferrari
43. all Andrea and Antonella Ferrari
44. Doug Perrine/Innerspace Visions
45. Bill Harrigan/Innerspace Visions
46. above Andrea and Antonella Ferrari
46. below Doug Perrine/Innerspace Visions
47. Doug Perrine/Innerspace Visions
48. Michele Hall/HHP
49. Bob Cranston/Innerspace Visions
50. Mark Conlin/Innerspace Visions
51. Mark Conlin/Innerspace Visions

52. all Andrea and Antonella Ferrari
53. above right Doug Perrine-José Castro/Inner-space Visions
53. belowAndrea and Antonella Ferrari
54. above Andrea and Antonella Ferrari
54. center Andrea and Antonella Ferrari
54. below Doug Perrine/Innerspace Visions
55. above left Doug Perrine/Innerspace Visions
55. above right Marty Snyderman/Innerspace Visions
55. below Marty Snyderman/Innerspace Visions
56. all Doug Perrine/Innerspace Visions
57. all Doug Perrine/Innerspace Visions
58. all Mark Conlin/Innerspace Visions
59. all Andrea and Antonella Ferrari
60. all Doug Perrine/Innerspace Visions
61. above right Doug Perrine/Innerspace Visions
61. center right Andrea and Antonella Ferrari
61. below right Doug Perrine/Innerspace Visions
62. all Doug Perrine/Innerspace Visions
63. all Doug Perrine/Innerspace Visions
64. Marty Snyderman
65. Doug Perrine/Innerspace Visions
66. Andrea and Antonella Ferrari
67. Marty Snyderman/Innerspace Visions
68. all Andrea and Antonella Ferrari
69. all Andrea and Antonella Ferrari
70. all Andrea and Antonella Ferrari
71. above Bob Cranston/Innerspace Visions
71. center right Andrea and Antonella Ferrari
71. below Andrea and Antonella Ferrari
72. Franklin Viola
73. Andrea and Antonella Ferrari
74. Andrea and Antonella Ferrari
75. above Andrea and Antonella Ferrari
75. below Doug Perrine/Innerspace Visions
76. Andrea and Antonella Ferrari
77. all Abdel-Rehman Al-Khathlan
78. Andrea and Antonella Ferrari
79. Andrea and Antonella Ferrari
80. all Andrea and Antonella Ferrari
81. all Andrea and Antonella Ferrari
82. all Andrea and Antonella Ferrari
83. all Andrea and Antonella Ferrari
84. all Andrea and Antonella Ferrari
85. Andrea and Antonella Ferrari
87. Antonio Busetto
88-9. Mark Conlin/Innerspace Visions
90-1. Marty Snyderman/Innerspace Visions
91. center Mark Conlin/Innerspace Visions
91. below Marty Snyderman/Innerspace Visions
92. above Rudie Kuiter/ Innerspace Visions
92. below Gwen Lowe/Innerspace Visions
93. all David B. Fleetham/Innerspace Visions
94. Florian Graner/Innerspace Visions
95. above Gwen Lowe/Innerspace Visions
95. below Richard Ellis/Innerspace Visions
96. above Gwen Lowe/Innerspace Visions
96. below David B. Fleetham/Innerspace Visions
97. Chris Huss/Innerspace Visions

98. all Marty Snyderman/Innerspace Visions
99. Mark Conlin/Innerspace Visions
100. all Rudie Kuiter/ Innerspace Visions
101. all Mark Conlin/Innerspace Visions
102. above Rudie Kuiter/ Innerspace Visions
102. below Mako Irose/Innerspace Visions
103. above Mark Conlin/Innerspace Visions
103. below Doug Perrine/Innerspace Visions
104. above David B. Fleetham/Innerspace Visions
104. below Norbert Wu/Innerspace Visions
105. Mark Conlin/Innerspace Visions
106-7. James D. Watt/Innerspace Visions
108-9. Andrea and Antonella Ferrari
108. above Andrea and Antonella Ferrari
109. center Mark Strickland/Innerspace Visions
109. below Andrea and Antonella Ferrari
110. all Rudie Kuiter/ Innerspace Visions
111. above Nigel Marsh/Innerspace Visions
111. below Marty Snyderman/Innerspace Visions
112. above Nigel Marsh/Innerspace Visions
112. center Norbert Wu/Innerspace Visions
113. above Marty Snyderman/Innerspace Visions
113. center Doug Perrine/Innerspace Visions
114. above David B. Fleetham/Innerspace Visions
114. center Nigel Marsh/Innerspace Visions
115. all Rudie Kuiter/ Innerspace Visions
116. above Scott W. Michael/ Innerspace Visions
116. below Mark Conlin/Innerspace Visions
117. all Scott W. Michael/Innerspace Visions
118. above David Hall/Innerspace Visions
118. below Scott W. Michael/Innerspace Visions
119. all Doug Perrine/Innerspace Visions
120. all Andrea and Antonella Ferrari
121. all Andrea and Antonella Ferrari
122. all Doug Perrine/Innerspace Visions
123. Doug Perrine/Innerspace Visions
124. all Andrea and Antonella Ferrari
125. all Andrea and Antonella Ferrari
126. Andrea and Antonella Ferrari
127. all Doug Perrin/Innerspace Visions
128-9. Doug Perrine/Innerspace Visions
130. above James D. Watt/Innerspace Visions
130-1. Bob Cranston/Innerspace Visions
132. all Doug Perrine/Innerspace Visions
133. all Doug Perrine/Innerspace Visions
134. all Juan Zumbado/Innerspace Visions
135. all David Shen/Innerspace Visions
136. Tom Haight/Innerspace Visions
137. all Andrea and Antonella Ferrari
138. all Howard Hall/Innerspace Visions
139. above Bob Cranston/Innerspace Visions
139. below Marty Snyderman/Innerspace Visions
140. above James D. Watt/Innerspace Visions
140. center Amos Nachoum/Innerspace Visions
141. James D. Watt/Innerspace Visions
142. above Jeff Rotman/Innerspace Visions
142. below David B. Fleetham/Innerspace Visions
143. above Mark Strickland/Innerspace Visions
143. below Dan Gotshall/Innerspace Visions
144-5. Richard Herrmann/Innerspace Visions

146-7. all Andrea and Antonella Ferrari
148. all Rudie Kuiter/ Innerspace Visions
149. all Mark Conlin/Innerspace Visions
150. above David B. Fleetham/Innerspace Visions
150. below Steve Drogin/Innerspace Visions
151. above Florian Graner/Innerspace Visions
151. below Don DeMaria/Innerspace Visions
152. above Don DeMaria/Innerspace Visions
152. below Doug Perrine/Innerspace Visions
153. above Don DeMaria/Innerspace Visions
153. below Doug Perrine/Innerspace Visions
154. all Doug Perrine/Innerspace Visions
155. Doug Perrine/Innerspace Visions
156. above David B. Fleetham/Innerspace Visions
156. below Doug Perrine/Innerspace Visions
157. Doug Perrine/Innerspace Visions
158. all Andrea and Antonella Ferrari
159. all Andrea and Antonella Ferrari
160. Nigel Marsh//Innerspace Visions
161. all Doug Perrine/Innerspace Visions
162. all Andrea and Antonella Ferrari
163. all Andrea and Antonella Ferrari
164. all David B. Fleetham/Innerspace Visions
165. all David B. Fleetham/Innerspace Visions
166. Doug Perrine/Innerspace Visions
167. all Doug Perrine/Innerspace Visions
168. all Doug Perrine/Innerspace Visions
169. above David B. Fleetham/Innerspace Visions
169. center Doug Perrine/Innerspace Visions
170. all Doug Perrine/Innerspace Visions
171. all Doug Perrine/Innerspace Visions
172. Andrea and Antonella Ferrari
173. all Andrea and Antonella Ferrari
174. above Doug Perrine/Innerspace Visions
174. below Masa Ushioda/Innerspace Visions
175. above Masa Ushioda/Innerspace Visions
175. below Doug Perrine/Innerspace Visions
176. all Doug Perrine/Innerspace Visions
177. all Doug Perrine/Innerspace Visions
178. all Doug Perrine/Innerspace Visions
179. all Doug Perrine/Innerspace Visions
180. Doug Perrine/Innerspace Visions
181. all Doug Perrine/Innerspace Visions
182. all Doug Perrine/Innerspace Visions
183. Richard Herrmann/Innerspace Visions
184. Bob Cranston/Innerspace Visions
185. all Doug Perrine/Innerspace Visions
186. all Andrea and Antonella Ferrari
187. all Andrea and Antonella Ferrari
188. above Doug Perrine/Innerspace Visions
188. below Andrea and Antonella Ferrari
189. Doug Perrine/Innerspace Visions
190. above Gary Adkison/Innerspace Visions
190. below Doug Perrine/Innerspace Visions
191. Doug Perrine/Innerspace Visions
192. all Doug Perrine/Innerspace Visions
193. above Doug Perrine/Innerspace Visions
193. center Rudie Kuiter/ Innerspace Visions
194-5. Marilyn Kazmers/Innerspace Visions
196. above Andrea and Antonella Ferrari

196. below Antonio Busetto
197. top Andrea and Antonella Ferrari
197. second down Doug Perrine/Innerspace Visions
197. third down David B. Fleetham/Innerspace Visions
197. fourth down Andrea and Antonella Ferrari
197. fifth down Andrea and Antonella Ferrari
198. Andrea and Antonella Ferrari
199. all Andrea and Antonella Ferrari
201. Antonio Busetto
202. Doug Perrine/Innerspace Visions
203. all Mark Strickland/Innerspace Visions
204. above Mark Strickland/Innerspace Visions
204. below Marty Snyderman/Innerspace Visions
205. Rudie Kuiter/Innerspace Visions
206. all Rudie Kuiter/Innerspace Visions
207. all Phillip Colla/Innerspace Visions
208. Doug Perrine/Innerspace Visions
209. all Doug Perrine/Innerspace Visions
210. above Mark Conlin/Innerspace Visions
210. below David B. Fleetham/Innerspace Visions
211. all Andrea and Antonella Ferrari
212. all Andrea and Antonella Ferrari
213. all Andrea and Antonella Ferrari
214. all Andrea and Antonella Ferrari
215. all Andrea and Antonella Ferrari
216. all Andrea and Antonella Ferrari
217. all Andrea and Antonella Ferrari
218. all Andrea and Antonella Ferrari
219. all Andrea and Antonella Ferrari
220. Nigel Marsh/Innerspace Visions
221. Nigel Marsh/Innerspace Visions
222. all Andrea and Antonella Ferrari
223. above Nigel Marsh/Innerspace Visions
223. below Andrea and Antonella Ferrari
224. above Andrea and Antonella Ferrari
224. below Rudie Kuiter/Innerspace Visions
225. Mike Johnson/Innerspace Visions
226. all Rudie Kuiter/Innerspace Visions
227. all Doug Perrine/Innerspace Visions
228. above Rudie Kuiter/Innerspace Visions
228. below Mark Conlin/Innerspace Visions
229. all Phillip Colla/Innerspace Visions
230. all Andrea and Antonella Ferrari
231. all Andrea and Antonella Ferrari
232. all David B. Fleetham/Innerspace Visions
233. Doug Perrine/Innerspace Visions
234. all Andrea and Antonella Ferrari
235. all Andrea and Antonella Ferrari
236. Andrea and Antonella Ferrari
237. Andrea and Antonella Ferrari
238. above Florian Graner/Innerspace Visions
238. below David B. Fleetham/ Innerspace Visions
239. all Rudie Kuiter/Innerspace Visions
240-1. Doug Perrine/Innerspace Visions

Cover photographs are by:
Andrea and Antonella Ferrari
Amos Nachoum/Innerspace Visions
Doug Perrine/Innerspace Visions
Marty Snyderman/Innerspace Visions